What people are saying about

Pathway to the Stable

In this rich and rewarding series of studies, Ivor Rees has taken us deep into the biblical world in order to show us once more the glory of the coming of Our Lord, the nativity and childhood of Jesus Christ. The context takes us back, to the Old Testament expectation and its messianic fulfilment, but the application is modern, showing us how relevant the story remains to the complexities and conundrums of twenty-first century life. Although rooted in scripture, the author knows that his witness and ours must always be for our own time and to our own world. The verse which occurred to me again and again as I read these chapters was 'Jesus Christ is the same yesterday and today and forever' (Hebrews 13: 8). It is a pleasure to commend this penetrating and heart-warming volume.

Revd. D. Densil Morgan, Professor of Theology, University of Wales Trinity Saint David

New light on an old story: A lifetime of Nativity plays could not prepare you for the twists and turns on the route to Bethlehem and back explored in Pathway to the Stable, a fascinating book that gives Christmas a contemporary realism. Only men needed to register in the census. So why did Joseph take a heavily pregnant Mary with him? Was he afraid to leave her with his family? Even to leave her with her own family? Was it the end of the story for the Wise Men – or the beginning? Almost 40 years later when evangelists travelled east to take the Good News, they were welcomed by people who had already been told. And a thousand years later, Marco Polo, claimed he was shown the tombs of the Magi. Was the temple visit of the 12-year-old Jesus the occasion of his Bar Mitzvah? On the long journey home it was common to walk in groups of men, boys, women, girls. H̶ the Bar Mitzvah group. His parents wo̶ families came together for the night. Thi

of history, literature, theology, language, culture, with seeming ease to shine a striking, modern light on the circumstances around the birth of Christ at the same time that it underlines the strong link between them and stories in the Old Testament.

Dr. Jean Silvan Evans, former Journalist & Lecturer in Journalism, elder of the United Reformed Church.

Ivor Thomas Rees' decades of pastoral ministry and years of study of Scripture are richly reflected in this beautiful new Advent resource for ministers and laypersons – and all those who seek the Holy Child of Bethlehem. Preachers will appreciate the depth of Biblical scholarship and vibrant interpretive work as they prepare for Advent and Christmas preaching, while lay readers will gain new and faith-filled insights and historical context for beloved Scripture we think we already know so well. Ivor Rees' writing style is warm and engaging; the author is both scholar and minister as he guides the reader through sacred texts and history, the fateful decisions ordinary people like Mary and Joseph made after encounters with God, and how these stories speak to us today. 'Pathway to the Stable' is clearly a labour of love for Ivor Rees, and a marvellous early Christmas present for all who are earnest about their faith in Jesus Christ.

The Revd. Kathy Lawes, Associate Conference Minister, Illinois Conference, United Church of Christ.

Pathway to the Stable offers a thoughtful, biblical and prayerful introduction to the Christmas story. Ivor Rees introduces us to the various characters, places and sources which are found in the Bible accounts, and draws them together to bring out the meaning of Jesus' birth at Bethlehem. I commend it to all who seek to delve deeper into these familiar stories and uncover more of the mystery of Christ's Incarnation.

Revd. Dr. Stephen Wigley, Chairman, Wales District of the Methodist Church.

This collection of portraits from the biblical birth narratives reflects a life-long commitment to a ministry of preaching and bible study. Here the familiar - perhaps over-familiar - characters are set within their religious and cultural context so as to reveal something of their significance within Jesus' story as well as ours. The short prayers at the end of each chapter help us to focus on the message for us. This short book would be a helpful guide for anyone wishing to use the period of Advent to seek new insights on familiar characters.

Revd. Dr. Noel Davies, former General Secretary, Cytun, Churches Together in Wales.

In this book we are given the kind of material we need for our meditations in the Christmas season. Light of touch and with pastoral concern, born of a lifetime of Christian ministry, the Revd. Ivor Thomas Rees challenges us to look afresh at passages of Scripture with which we can at times be overfamiliar. Above all, there are riches here for mind and spirit, as we try to make our way 'even unto Bethlehem and see this thing which has come to pass.

Ceri Davies, Emeritus Professor of Classics, an elder of the Presbyterian Church of Wales.

Routinely, the secular world introduces Christmas on the shelves of supermarkets sometime in October. A month or so later the church constantly seeks ways to slow down that marketing mania by encouraging a careful observance of Advent. In this very readable book Ivor Rees provides a useful resource to help us as individuals to 'slow down' as we rediscover annually our own 'pathways to the stable'. It leaves no Christmas stone unturned as its makes significant connections between scripture, tradition, personalities and questions in preparation for the birthday of our Lord.

The Ven. Andrew Carrol Jones, Archdeacon of Merioneth, author and regular contributor to *New Daylight*.

Ivor Rees writes informatively and reflectively about the Christmas story, in ways that will give new depth of insight to many readers. He has done his homework, and gives a good deal of background on people and places in those early chapters of Matthew and Luke. More than this, Ivor's writing also draws out a message of faith for Christians today, so that the events and texts speak into our own experience. Telling of Christmas in these ways puts flesh on the ancient word.

The Revd. Dr. John Proctor, General Secretary, United Reformed Church.

Here is a gem from one who throughout a long ministry has taught and preached the meaning of the Incarnation. In this book his thoughts are crystallised providing us with valuable historical, theological and spiritual insights into the Christmas story.

The Revd. Canon Arthur Howells, author of *The Little Book of Advent*, and *The Little Book of Lent*.

In this companion book to his work on the passion, Ivor sees Christmas and Easter as part of one action. He draws on his years as a United Reformed Church minister preaching about Christmas and considers the historical aspects, but through his questions about the characters in the narrative he also invites us to consider their motivation, and by ending each chapter with a prayer, he helps us to consider how we might be God-enablers and God-bearers in our place and time.

The Revd. Simon Walkling, Moderator of the National Synod of Wales, United Reformed Church

Pathway to
the Stable

Pathway to the Stable

Ivor Thomas Rees

Winchester, UK
Washington, USA

First published by Circle Books, 2018
Circle Books is an imprint of John Hunt Publishing Ltd., No. 3 East St., Alresford,
Hampshire SO24 9EE, UK
office1@jhpbooks.net
www.johnhuntpublishing.com
www.circle-books.com

For distributor details and how to order please visit the 'Ordering' section on our website.

Text copyright: Ivor Thomas Rees 2017

ISBN: 978 1 78535 860 9
978 1 78535 861 6 (ebook)
Library of Congress Control Number: 2017954132

A CIP catalogue record for this book is available from the British Library.

Design: Stuart Davies

Printed and bound by CPI Group (UK) Ltd, Croydon, CR0 4YY, UK

We operate a distinctive and ethical publishing philosophy in
all areas of our business, from our global network of authors to
production and worldwide distribution.

Contents

Books by Ivor Thomas Rees
Welsh Hustings 1885-2004 (2005)
Saintly Enigma (2011)
Yr Wythnos Honno (2011)
Pathway to the Cross (2012)
The Sledgehammer Pastor (2015)
Clapham Dissenters (2015)
Y Noson Honno (2016)

To Delyth
The Revd. Leslie Jane Noon and Mr. Geoff Noon
And the members of the Uniting Church, Sketty, Swansea

Foreword

This book looks at the 'dramatis personae' surrounding the birth of Jesus – a kind of story of Christmas told from the edges. There are insights into the characters of Zechariah, John, Mary and Joseph to name but a few and each chapter begins with a verse or two from scripture and ends with a short and purposeful prayer. It gathers information from a variety of sources, biblical, historical (e.g. Dialogue with Trypho, the works of Josephus) and linguistic (Greek words like thaumazein are explained). It draws on an Ignatian approach as the author imagining himself at the various scenes in the story. He uses personal and contemporary analogies to lend immediacy to the narrative. He also imparts impressive geographical knowledge, suggesting two places known today where Mary might have met the angel Gabriel: at the site of the 1769 Orthodox Church of St Gabriel or the Catholic Basilica of the Annunciation. It offers some rich detail: for example, John the Baptist may have had links with the independent Essenes; the three-strong Magi of Caspar, Melchior and Balthazar, though not named in scripture, may have derived from India, Persia and Arabia respectively; the word 'Nazorite' may be etymologically rooted in the Jewish word 'to consecrate'. The Epilogue then introduces us to the starting-points of each of the Gospels, as if to say that the scene is now set for Jesus' adult ministry – and for our discipleship to begin - so challenging us to think about what it might mean.

Most. Revd. Dr. Barry Morgan, Archbishop of Wales 2003-2016

Foreword

What wonderful memories I have of childhood Christmases – remembering each one as better than the last, with all the excitement of wrapping presents and hiding secrets, the anticipation of waiting, and the activity of preparation, coming together in the days of fun and festival. I realise now that it was so good because it all made sense to me as a child – I knew what we were celebrating. I had been told the Jesus story and caught the mystery of God's love, experienced in my family, among my friends and in the church. We shared the Jesus story together and seemed to know what it meant for our lives today. Sadly in the 50 years since, the Christian festival has been buried under an avalanche of tinsel and glitter. The Christmas season gets longer, the food consumed ever greater, the partying more an alcoholic stupor, and the family's debt more crippling. It all seems to be disguising an emptiness of spirit, as we have forgotten, or never knew why the celebrations.

How timely is *Pathway to the Stable*! Ivor Rees invites us on this journey of discovery of the riches of the Christmas story. Ivor invites us to join those who were on that first journey to Bethlehem, to meet Jesus' family, including the aunts and uncles – those invited to the party, but also some unexpected guests such as nearby shepherds, probably unwashed and certainly common-spoken, and strangers from foreign lands, probably wealthy and certainly clever-spoken. Ivor doesn't leave us in Bethlehem, for we will be taken to the holy place to meet the saintly, and also to the palace to meet the ungodly. We join the family on a scary escape as refugees and then the adventure of bringing up their child. The climax of the journey is to hear again what all this means for the world in the fanfare of John's opening words to his gospel, and then, breathlessly invited to join the adult Jesus in his mission, as recorded in Mark, like answering the bugle to wake up to God's service.

So, be prepared for the journey, for nor does Ivor leave us 2000 years ago, but this book speaks into our lives today. I am sure, that for many there will be a rediscovery of what we were taught, but each of us will also discover new understanding and see new perspectives of the Christmas story. This book is an ideal accompaniment to an advent preparation, with Ivor's perceptive questions drawing out a 21st Century response. Use them in your private study and prayers, or I would hope, many churches will use them collectively to share our responses and our experiences. Reading *Pathway to the Stable* is like receiving the gift of a railway ticket home, to join the family again for a true Christ-centred Christmas celebration. Enjoy the Feast!

The Revd. Kevin Watson, Moderator of the General Assembly of the United Reformed Church, 2016-2018.

Preface

These eighteen years of retirement have proved a time of blessing as well as of enjoyment. The only times in a year when I really miss being minister of a church are during Holy Week/Easter and at Christmas. Sunday, 6 October 2013 marked the retirement of the Revd. Kim Fabricius from the pastorate of Bethel United Reformed Church, Sketty, Swansea, where he had exercised an outstanding ministry since his ordination in 1982. On the following Sunday the Bethel congregation began worshipping each Sunday with the congregation of Sketty Methodist Church and sharing the weekday activities, as we went through the process of becoming a local ecumenical partnership. Then, in May 2015, the Uniting Church, Sketty, came into being. This has been a wonderful time, greatly appreciated all the members of this new congregation of Christ's people. We have been richly blessed by the ministry of the Revd. Lesley Noon, who came to Sketty from Huddersfield in 2013 to lead us in our pilgrimage.

Nonetheless, at Christmas I still miss the in-depth preparation involved for Advent and Christmas worship.

Perhaps it was that which impelled into thinking of writing this book on Christmas, following on *Pathway to the Cross*, published in 2012. I can but pray that reading it will prove something of the same blessing as researching and writing it.

It was suggested that I added questions at the end of each chapter in case readers or groups wished to discuss them.

Ivor Thomas Rees

Thanks

As usual I am indebted to many people: to the people whose names appear on the rear cover, who provided not only their kind words but very helpful comment and advice; to daughter Lythan and son-in-law Phil Nevard, for also giving me the run of the more modern library at Christmas, and especially, as usual, to Delyth for her patient editing and help.

Sweet Child of Bethlehem, grant that we may share with all our hearts in this profound mystery of Christmas. Pour into the hearts of men and women the peace which they sometimes seek so desperately, and which you alone can give them. Help them to know one another better, and to live as sisters and brothers, children of the same Father. Awaken in their hearts and ours love and gratitude for your infinite goodness. Join us all in your love and give us your heavenly peace.

Pope John XXIII

Chapter One

Belonging

In thy seed shall all the nations of the earth be blessed; because
thou hast obeyed my voice.
(Genesis 23.18)

It has been said that when one meets an Englishman, if he asks
a question it will be about the nature of one's work or business.
My own experience tells me that, though this can be the case, it
is far from being a universal truth. Television drama suggests
that perhaps the aristocracy is more concerned with family and
blood. Members of other nations, including the Welsh, will begin
with "Where are you from?" followed by "Who do you belong
to?" This concern for relationship is to be found too among the
Jews and other ancient peoples. Thus, Paul describes himself as
"a member of the people of Israel, of the tribe of Benjamin, a
Hebrew born of the Hebrews." Kinship was important and each
family needed to know and declare its ancestral pedigree for
such knowledge was the basis of all social relationship.

Matthew sets out the genealogy of Jesus through Joseph's
line, a chapter rarely read but deserving of better treatment. In
beginning with the phrase "book of the generations," Matthew is
following a pattern to be found in the Book of Genesis. Chapter
5 opens with "the list of the descendants of Adam" and its list
of generations leads to Noah, "a righteous man, blameless in
his generation. Noah walked with God." Noah was God's agent
of the new beginning for the human race after the flood and
thus a prototype of the Saviour who was to come. Matthew's
account sets out the generations: from Abraham to David with a
list of patriarchs, David to the Exile, listing kings, and the Exile
to Christ, giving the names of individuals, suggesting that the

revelation of God's plan of redemption continues through each epoch. The call of Abraham marks a new beginning after Babel and reaches its climax in David. Then come the events leading to the Exile. The return from Exile is another new beginning, reaching its climax in the coming of Christ. Three kings are omitted from the list – Ahaziah, Joseph and Amaziah – these were not of the house of David, indeed, they were opposed to it.

Surprisingly, there are four women: Tamar (Genesis 38. 11ff), Rahab the harlot (Joshua 6. 17, 22-25), Ruth the Moabitess (Ruth) and Bethsheba (2 Samuel 11-12), wife of Uriah the Hittite. These are not only female but also foreign and the relationships of all four were unusual. What is stressed is that each of these women either kept the Covenant or entered into it by an act of faith. God's kingdom is based on his covenant of grace and is open to women and foreigners on equal terms, to pagans and prostitutes alike.

Matthew is concerned to tell his readers, Jewish Christians, that Jesus is the anointed King, of the royal line of David and Israel's promised Messiah. Jesus is too the descendant of Abraham, the Father of the People, by whom all the nations of earth are to be blessed. This evangelist is concerned to explain why Gentiles are to have a place in the Kingdom of Heaven and therefore among God's people on earth. He is preparing the way for his record of the denunciation of the Pharisees and Sadducees by John the Baptist (3.7-10): 'Do not presume to say to yourselves, "We have Abraham as our ancestor," for I tell you, God is able from these stones to raise up children to Abraham,"' as well as the declaration by Jesus in the story of the centurion's servant (Matthew 8.5-13) that "many will come from east and west and will eat with Abraham, Isaac and Jacob in the kingdom of heaven, while the heirs of the kingdom will be thrown into outer darkness." Matthew is concerned to stress that the news he records is the fulfilment of the eternal purposes of God. So, in 1.22-23, he quotes Isaiah 7.14: "Look, the virgin shall conceive and bear a son, and they shall name him Emmanuel." On at least three other occasions in the first two chapters he refers to Scripture to confirm what he is claiming. There are, too, close resemblances between the flight into Egypt and its return with the story of Moses (see chapter 12). Christ sacrifices relationship with God, family and the respectable for the sake of outsiders.

Whereas Matthew opens his Gospel with his genealogy table, Luke places his account between that of the Baptism of Jesus and his temptation in the wilderness. Luke works backwards from Joseph to Adam, through Nathan, a less important son to his father David and on through Jacob, Isaac and Abraham, through Shem, Noah and Seth to Adam. It has been suggested that his purpose in working this way is to draw his readers' immediate attention to Jesus himself. The lists between Abraham and David are almost identical but are vastly different from David to Joseph; in this section only two names appear on both lists, those of Shealtiel and Zerubbabel. The differences in these two genealogies have caused debate among scholars down the ages, especially since such details were usually painstakingly recorded by Jewish scribes. For example, it was said at Tantur in 1989 that there was a Jewish family in Galilee which had never left its village, which could trace its ancestry back to around 150 B.C.

Luke's list begins at Luke 3.23 with "He [Joseph] was the son (as was thought) of Heli..." This creates a problem from the start because Matthew 1.16 declares: "and Jacob the father of Joseph, the husband of Mary, of whom Jesus was born, who is called the Christ." One of the earlier theories explains this by the tradition of "Levirite marriage," whereby if two brothers live together and one dies, leaving no son to succeed him; his brother would marry the widow to provide sons to carry on the name and line of the deceased brother (Deuteronomy 25.5-10). By this, Joseph was the legal son of Heli, who had died, and the natural son of Jacob. By this theory, Joseph's grandfathers - Luke's 'Matthat' and Matthew's 'Matthan' - are brothers, both of whom married the same woman, so that Matthat's son (Heli) is the legal father of Joseph and Matthan his natural father. Perhaps such theorising is really beside the point. Martin Luther said that Joseph's line is recorded by Matthew and that of Mary by Luke whilst Julius Africanus suggested that, as has been noted, Matthew follows the natural line and Luke the legal.

The evangelists' concern with ancestry was quite common in the ancient world and is still important in many parts of the world. Being able to recite the names of your forefathers was proof of belonging. Being "one of us, not one of them" was essential for survival. Questions of status too were settled by reference to ancestry. Ezra 2.62 tells of the search for proof of priestly status after the return from exile: "They looked for their entries in the genealogical records but they were not there and were excluded from the priesthood as unclean."

Both Matthew and Luke, however, though setting out to present history, are concerned with more than history. Both are concerned with the kerygma, the proclamation of the Gospel. Jesus is not another pagan demi-god; he is a human being, with a human family. He is the Son of David the King, a claim repeated in the New Testament. This is stressed by both evangelists, who also state that Jesus is the son of Abraham. This is Matthew's main concern in beginning the family tree with Abraham. For Matthew and his Jewish readers, this Jesus is a human being, the Son of David the King and the Son of Abraham, father of the people, but for Matthew he is too the Son of God, the Christ/ Promised Saviour and Emmanuel, "God with us." It is worth noting that Matthew uses the phrase 'Son of David" ten times, more than the total usage by Mark and Luke put together, whilst the phrase is totally absent from John's Gospel.

Luke's birth narrative tells us that Jesus is the son of Mary, who is also of the house and lineage of David and a descendant of Abraham but he takes us back to Adam, "the father of us all," and through Adam to God. Jesus is the Son of Man and Saviour of all humanity. The central declaration of both writers is that Jesus, Lord and Redeemer, is the Son of God. He has come to bring God's wandering children back into his family, part of a redeemed creation.

It seems to be that the sense of belonging has weakened considerably during the last century. Young people leave home for university or work and often do not return home permanently. The strong sense of community to be found in the South Wales mining valleys, though still, perhaps, stronger than in other, more prosperous places, is nonetheless not what it was. One of the great concerns of the Christmas which is just past is that one million pensioners spent the holiday in loneliness. Another sign of this is the fact that a large amount of British new housing is aimed to young people who choose to live alone. Hearing the pensioners' story made me say that at least belonging to a church provides a sense of belonging but then I recalled being in a crowded church on Christmas morning where people seemed very friendly to each other but ignored us completely.

God our Father: your Son Jesus Christ became a human being to claim us human beings as sisters and brothers in faith. Make us one with him, so that we may enjoy your love, and, as he lived, so may we live in joyful service as your children; for the sake of him who lives and reigns with you and the Holy Spirit, one God, now and forever.

Questions for thought or discussion
1. How important, especially for Christians, is a sense of belonging to others?
2. One church secretary wrote of meetings which attracted "the right sort of people." What is the significance for us of Tamar the Harlot, Ruth the Moabitess and Bathsheba, listed in the genealogies or of Mary Magdalene, Matthew

the tax-collector and Simon the leper?

3. Can a true Christian community be unwelcoming to strangers and outsiders?

Chapter Two

Prototypes and Promises

These all died in faith, not having received the promises, but having seen them from afar off were assured of them, embraced them, and confessed that they were strangers and pilgrims on earth... Therefore God is not ashamed to be called their God, for he has prepared a city for them. (Hebrews 11.13)

Doubtless, we have all met people who decided to have a go at reading the Bible by starting with Genesis because that is the first book in the volume as it has come down to us. They planned to read straight through, only to get bogged down sooner or later in the Old Testament. However, editorial order is not everything. The Hebrew understanding of God began with the people's experience of his involvement in their exodus from Egypt. It was that experience which started their relationship with God and their questioning search to know him better and understand him more fully. The Hebrew Bible is the record of that search and that relationship.

Christians need to read their Scriptures in a Christian way so that the Christian starting point for Bible reading is not the Old Testament but a gospel, probably that of Mark. What is even more wrong for a Christian than starting with Genesis is believing that Christians do not need the Old Testament. The Old Testament is essential to our understanding of the incarnation of Jesus Christ and the whole of the message of the New Testament. At the same time, the key to understanding the Old Testament is Jesus Christ. Saint Augustine the Great speaks for the early Christian Fathers in his statement that "the New Testament is the consummation or fulfilment of the Old." Thus the Old Testament needs to be read in the light of its fulfilment in Jesus Christ. When that happens, then Jesus appears in all sorts of unexpected places.

Genesis 1.31 portrays the last day of the creation: "God saw everything that he had made and indeed, it was very good." The final words can mean "completely perfect." What is God seeing here? Is it what happened by the end of the sixth day? Or is God looking through all the process of creation to its final fulfilment? Does the picture include the whole sweep of world history as presented in the Scriptures? The rest of the Bible story is to do with human failure and God's grace – his love for those who have no claim on it, who do not deserve it – and the way in which that grace leads to final victory and fulfilment of divine purpose. John opens his gospel with the trumpet sound of his Prologue, where he calls Christ the Word, declaring that the Word was there at the beginning, when God spoke and creation came about.

The Hebrew Bible, which became for Christians the Old Testament, tells of the preparation for the coming of the Saviour of the world. The God who saw "that everything was very good" was active throughout the biblical story in working to ensure that it was to be so in the final fulfilment of his purpose. The redemption of humanity is set out early on in that story, with constant pointers to how it is to be brought about through the incarnation, death and resurrection of Jesus Christ, Son of God and Son of Man.

We can find pointers to Christ in events and festivals. The God met in the Exodus is found to be Lord of nature and history; he judges tyrants and is merciful to his people, with whom he creates a covenant relationship. The lambs slaughtered at Passover point to the Lamb of God, "with all the marks of slaughter on him" and "slain from the foundation of the world."

The unleavened (flawless) bread of the Exodus becomes the Bread of Life, broken for us. Christ is the first fruit, sown for a great harvest. His power and glory were seen at Pentecost, when his Spirit filled the temple, a promise that later that same Spirit would overflow out into the world, fifty days after the resurrection of Christ.

The gospels seem to suggest that the coming of Christ in the fifteenth year of the reign of Tiberius was a sudden event, long awaited but then unexpected whereas, in fact, the incarnation followed on an ages-long process of preparation of his way. The accounts of Mary, Joseph and the shepherds tell of surprise and amazement but the magi, like the elderly Simeon and Anna, point to searching and faithful waiting.

It was by the Word that God spoke as he walked with Adam in the garden, that he led Noah into the ark, that he made a covenant with Abraham. This is how he called to Moses from the burning bush, divided the Red Sea, led the people through the wilderness and gave them the Law at Sinai. He spoke with patriarchs, kings and prophets and to common people. They became the instruments of his purpose. None of these may be called a 'plaster-saint'. All are human, with foibles and faults but all respond to the call of God with greater or lesser faith and obedience. They contain three basic types: the first two contain prototypes of Jesus, whose lives point to something in the story of Christ; the second group declares the promises of God, which are fulfilled in the person of Jesus Christ, whilst the last group contains those people who are faithful, whatever befalls them: in the New Testament such people are called "the saints." We meet some of their sort in the evangelist's accounts of the Nativity.

Who are some of these prototypes? Abraham responded without hesitation to the call of God to leave home and go on a journey not knowing where he went, as the first to walk the missionary road of God. Where he goes, what he does and what he experiences is for the good of others: "Go from your country and your kindred and your father's house... I will make of you a great nation... and in you all the families of the earth will be blessed. So Abram went..."[1] God calls a man, who is released from all tribal ties and sent to be the father of a new nation, through which the whole human race is to be blessed through all generations. The Tower of Babel story reveals the human tendency to create "us and them." This time it is a united race which seeks independence of God and that leads to ruin. The calling of this one man and the covenant made with him gives hope for all the world, a hope which is fulfilled in a son of Abraham, who takes on himself all the sin and sorrow of the world and carries it to his cross for the salvation of all the world. Just as Lot is saved because of Abraham, so the world is saved because of Jesus. The prophets Isaiah and Zechariah take up the theme in Abraham's calling. It is repeated on at least three occasions in the New Testament.

Joseph incurred the anger of his brothers, who sold him at a price into slavery in Egypt, where he endured cruelty and hardship, before being exalted to the king's right hand. He ensured that there was bread in Egypt. All of this was for the sake of the salvation of his father, brothers and their descendants, and through them the whole human family, to whom and for whom Christ came as the Saviour and Bread of Life.

The Book of Exodus opens with a new era. Joseph is dead and forgotten. A new king fears the growth of this immigrant Hebrew population and enslaves it. Still afraid, he orders the drowning in the Nile of every new-born Hebrew boy. The unsung heroines of that story are the midwives who disobey. Then a Levite woman gives birth to a boy, who is hidden in a basket, which is placed among the reeds of the Nile, until he is discovered and adopted by the king's daughter. He lives with an alien people as their prince, until he realises one day that he belongs with the enslaved nation. Moses is forced to flee into the wilderness from which God calls him, having "heard their groaning... and remembered his covenant with Abraham, Isaac and Jacob."[2] Moses is told to leave the wilderness and return to Egypt to lead the people out. On the wilderness journey he suffers abuse and death threats from those called to be the people of God, but his trust is in that same God. The parallels with the story of Jesus, the final Saviour, are strikingly clear. Moses dies on the banks of the Jordan and Joshua is the chosen one to lead the people across to take possession of the Promised Land. The sign that God is there is the Ark of the Covenant which will lead them through the water.

The story of Samuel and his mother Hannah also provides a prototype, as will be noted later in the birth narratives. The prophet Elijah leads the struggle against the followers of Baal, led by Ahab the king and his queen, Jezebel. This prophet too goes through a wilderness experience where, in his isolation, he hears the voice of God. The prophets who followed claimed a spiritual kinship with him through his disciple Elisha. Later generations looked to his return before the expected day of the Lord, when he would be an instrument of reconciliation.[3] The last of the prototype figures is David the King, who frees the nation from foreign threat and establishes a great kingdom. He too endures a wilderness period but his psalms show his faith in God, whom he never ceases to praise. His name appears more than eight hundred times in the Old Testament and sixty times in the New.

In the Old Testament story the word covenant appears in God's dealings with his servants. Several Hebrew words are used for covenant in the Old Testament, the most common appearing 286 times.[4] When it appears in the writings of the prophets, it is usually to do with the people's breaking of the covenant and God's judgement. Three speak of the hope given by a promised new covenant: '"The days are surely coming," says the Lord, "when I will make a new covenant with the house of Israel and the house of Judah."'[5] A covenant was made with Noah as he prepared the Ark, the sign of new beginning for the whole creation, including all its creatures.[6] The Book of Exodus tells how God heard the groaning of his people, "and

God remembered his covenant with Abraham, Isaac and Jacob."[7] Moses is made the messenger of covenant, which is renewed with the people at Sinai.[8] As has been noted, it was the Ark of the Covenant, which led the people through the Jordan. David on his death bed declares: "Is not my house like this with God? For he has made with me an everlasting covenant, ordered in all things and secure." The word appears also twenty times in the Psalms, in at least three of which the Lord remembers his covenant.[9]

The Old Testament story speaks of God's initiative, of his grace and favour, of the people's rejection of God, of judgement, forgiveness and restoration. Isaiah, in the first section of the book bearing his name (chapters 1-39), declares the sovereignty and holiness of God. It speaks of human sin and of faith in the Lord, of a faithful remnant and of the promise of the Messiah. The middle section (40-55), sometimes called Second or Deutero Isaiah, in the sixth century BC, proclaims a coming deliverance and a pardoning of guilt. A highway is to be built across the desert from Babylon for the coming of the Lord and all humanity will witness his glory. The first readers would be familiar with the maintenance of roads in that empire for any journey the king would wish to make. For Christians, the important passages here are those known as the Servant Songs or Songs of the Suffering Servant. The first (42.1-4, linked to 5-9) speaks of the gentleness and power of the Servant, who will "bring forth justice in the earth and the coastlands wait for his teaching." The Servant is given "as a covenant to the people, a light to the nations; to open the eyes that are blind, to bring out the prisoners from the dungeon, from the prison those who sit in darkness." The servants of God are blind to God; those in exile are like heart-broken prisoners. Their condition is due not to the world power which conquered them but to their own sin. The New Testament tells that Christ, the Light of the world, frees them and restores their sight through his own suffering. The second Servant Song follows similar themes, though its words are placed in the Servant's mouth. He has been called before he was born to be the servant of the Lord but feels that all his efforts have been in vain, "yet surely my cause is with the Lord, and my reward with my God." The second set of verses declares that he was sent to bring back the Lord's people but, more than that, he is to be "a light to the nations that my salvation may reach to the end of the earth." To the Redeemer, "despised and abhorred by the nations," kings and princes "shall prostrate themselves." Again there is reference to one "given as a covenant to the people," who releases "those who are in darkness" and who will feed the people, who are brought from every direction, on the highways to God. The other songs are concerned more with the Servant's sufferings. The third (50.4-11) describes how the obedient Servant is mocked and ill-treated by those he has come to save. It is the fourth song (Isaiah 52.13-53) which delves most deeply into the Servant's sufferings: "despised and rejected by men, a man of sorrows and acquainted with grief." "But he was wounded for our transgressions... by his stripes we are healed." The Lamb of God is led to the slaughter and makes no sound, but by his sufferings God's universal salvation is wrought.

The second great prophet of this century is Jeremiah, a man deeply aware of his call to proclaim the word of the Lord. His message of judgement with its call to repentance is opposed by the popular 'prophets' of his day and .he is not only rejected but beaten, imprisoned and threatened with death. When Judah falls, he shares in the suffering of his people. Eventually, in Chapters 30-31, known as "the Little Book of Comfort," there is hope. God will bring home his people, as a shepherd guides his flock. He will make a new covenant with his people, writing it upon their hearts. The cry of the Lamentations is akin to that of Jesus over Jerusalem on Palm Sunday.[10]

The third great prophet is Ezekiel, member of a priestly family. Called by God at the age of 30, he, like Jeremiah, proclaims the destruction of Jerusalem and its temple, for which he suffered opposition. Some twenty years after the opening of his ministry, he began to have visions of a new temple, a theme taken up in Hebrews 10.19-23: "since we have confidence to enter the sanctuary by the blood of Jesus, by the new and living way he has opened for us through the curtain (that is, through his flesh), and since we have a great high priest over the house of God, let us approach with a true heart in full assurance of faith, with our hearts sprinkled clean from an evil conscience and our bodies washed with pure water. Let us hold fast to the confession of our hope without wavering, for he who has promised is faithful."

The so-called "Minor Prophets" all look forward. The Book of Daniel, set in Babylon, speaks of conflict. Its message is that God, who saves Daniel and his companions, will save his people. Hosea uses his own suffering caused by his wife's infidelity and his redeeming her from slavery, to illustrate God's relationship with his people before turning to a moving picture of a father-son relationship. Joel forecasts the Day of the Lord, whilst Amos declares judgement and redemption. Jonah speaks of God's concern for the nations and his people disobedience in not sharing his justice. There is a kind of death and resurrection and the story ends with the triumphant mercy of God. Micah's words contain a pattern of doom and hope. Unjust rulers are condemned; the rights of the poor are defended and justice is proclaimed. The prophet looks forward to the restoration of God's people and universal peace, established by a Davidic king, who will come from Bethlehem of Ephrathah.[11] Zephaniah too proclaims the Day of the Lord, when all the nations will be brought to judgement. He foresees God's Kingdom, into which all the nations shall come, with the Lord himself present among them. Haggai prophesies the overthrow of the kingdoms, with all their might, and the establishment of a new temple. Zechariah, writing during the reign of the Persian king Darius and after the people's return to Jerusalem, records a series of visions.

He records the coming of the king who rides on a donkey, a passage quoted by the evangelists in their descriptions of Jesus' Palm Sunday procession. He will destroy weapons of war and establish peace for the nations, which will become the Kingdom of God. Malachi is the last book in the Old Testament. Parts of it are very similar to chapters in Zechariah. Malachi is concerned with the state of religion and ethics in post-exilic Jerusalem. He criticises the people for questioning the justice of God and calls on them to be faithful as they await its coming. Malachi promises the coming of the Day of the Lord, whose messenger will come to his temple, to purify priests and people but before his coming, God will send the prophet Elijah, a promise seen by Christians as referring to Christ and his forerunner John the Baptist.

It is the whole Bible which sets out the story of the world's redemption. The Old Testament is not merely the preface to the New but the first part of the total history. What begins in the Old Testament is fulfilled in the New. The incarnation of Christ as set out in the gospels is where that fulfilment begins.

God, for whom we wait, Keep us by your grace as we look
to your coming. May we be faithful in all things that we may
welcome you with joy and praise.

Questions for thought or discussion

1. What is the importance of the Old Testament for Christians?
2. Are there prophets now? If so, who are they?
3. Where is the redeeming work of Christ to be seen today?
4. What is our role?

Chapter Three

Cousin John

Behold, I will send my messenger, and he shall prepare the way before me; and the Lord, whom ye seek, shall suddenly come to his temple, even the messenger of the covenant, whom ye delight in: behold, he shall come, saith the Lord of hosts.
(Malachi 3.1)

It may seem strange that Luke begins his Gospel not with information about Jesus but with the birth of his cousin John Bar Zechariah, known as "The Baptist," but what Luke does is place the birth of the forerunner before that of the Messiah. John is the son of Zechariah, a priest of the order of Abijah, and of Elizabeth, a descendent of Aaron," all of whose male descendants were priests. This makes John a descendent of Aaron through both parents. Husband and wife are described as "righteous before God, living blamelessly according to all the commandments and regulations of the Lord." It is likely, despite their character and status, that they were the objects of some scorn for Elizabeth, was barren and they were both old.

By this time, there were some twenty thousand priests, so many that they were organised into twenty four groups, each of which served in the Temple for one week, twice a year. The only occasions on which all priests came to the Temple were at the feasts of Passover, Pentecost and Tabernacles. Most priests lived in towns within reach of Jerusalem. The town of Ein Karem, south west of Jerusalem, is said to be the home of Zechariah and Elizabeth. Not every priest actually had the possibility of fulfilling his priestly role by offering the morning or evening sacrifice at the altar, for that privilege was decided by lot. No priest was allowed to do this more than once in his life.

Zechariah is told that his prayer has been heard and his aged wife Elizabeth is to give birth to a son, to be called John, suggesting that while the priest was speaking the traditional words of the Jewish liturgy, his heart was crying out for a son. The fulfillment of this promise will give them "joy and gladness", which will be shared by many. The boy "will be great in the sight of the Lord." Though not called to take vows as a Nazarite[12] he is to be brought up in strict dedication to the Lord, totally abstaining from wine and strong drink. Zechariah's son is destined to be an important servant of the Lord. He will be the messenger promised by Malachi 3.1. He will be "filled with the Holy Spirit" and is destined to be the second Elijah, possessed of "the spirit and power" of the first of the great prophets. The words "He will turn the hearts of the fathers to the children" are a direct quote from the last sentence of Malachi's prophecies. Luke adds "and the disobedient to the wisdom of the just." At first sight, it appears to say that fathers will turn to their children and the children to their fathers. However, Luke says that whilst the Jews, for the most part, rejected the Messiah when he came, many Gentiles, the new children of Abraham, accepted him.[13] All of this is to prepare the people for the coming of the Messiah.

This proves too far-fetched for Zechariah, who is unable to believe his ears and he asks for proof. Here he is in company with his fellow Jews, who always ask for a sign to prove that something is true.[14] Zechariah is told that he is addressing Gabriel, who stands "in the presence of God," who has been sent to bring him this good news. His doubt is unacceptable, particularly here, perhaps, in this holy place where he is performing his priestly function. The priest is to be struck dumb until the promise is fulfilled and, as it became necessary to communicate with him by signs, he must have become deaf also.

Meanwhile, the congregation is becoming restless as it wonders what is keeping the priest and holding up the worship.

Eventually he appears, unable both to pronounce the Aaronic blessing and to explain what has happened. They realise that he has seen a vision. Luke ends this section quite prosaically, merely stating that when his week of service was at an end, the priest returned home. There Elizabeth receives no angelic message but she conceives, and spends five months in seclusion. There is no record of legal precept or custom for this. It may well be that because of her advanced age she wished to conceal herself. In the sixth month her cousin Mary is told of her condition.

Eventually the time of waiting is fulfilled and the child is born. Her neighbours rejoiced with the mother at this great blessing. At the baby's circumcision on his eighth day the child is to receive his name. It seems appropriate to name him after his father but Elizabeth objects, saying that his name is to be John (meaning *God's gift* or *God is gracious*). That is not good enough for those responsible for the circumcision and so they make signs to the father, who writes the word John. And immediately (a popular word in the New Testament) Zechariah's speech is restored and he praises God. Those present are filled with fear and they wonder what this is all about. "What will this child be?" And the story spread all around the region.

The Holy Spirit fills Zechariah with the gift of prophecy and his words have become another of the great hymns of the Church, known as *the Benedictus*. This is the first of three great songs to be found in Luke's account of the birth of Jesus.[15] It contains a number of Old Testament quotations.[16] Zechariah's song gives praise for the Messiah of the House of David, who will redeem his people from their foreign yoke as he promised to Abraham. The final section, verses 76-79 contains specific Christian content. This boy will "be called the prophet of the Most High, for you will go before the Lord to prepare his way." It is in this context that mention is made of 'salvation' and 'forgiveness of sins'. John is to preach repentance and redemption "through the tender mercy of our God." Zechariah echoes the declaration in Isaiah 9.2 (prophetic perfect) that "the people who walk in darkness have seen a great light." To darkness, Zechariah adds "the shadow of death." Darkness and death are overcome by him who will "guide our feet into the way of peace." For Zechariah God's promise has been fulfilled.

Even less is known of the early years of John the Baptist than of his cousin Jesus. What career did the elderly parents envisage for their baby son? With a priest for a father and a mother from a priestly family, priesthood would have seemed obvious. Probably, his father imagined him being a priest, a special priest who would proclaim the coming of the Lord, and with Elijah-like ardour and oratory, would win back thousands to the faith of their fathers, but it is an understatement to say that he chose not to go down that path. As the child of elderly parents it seems obvious that he would be orphaned at an early age. His nurture would have been in the hands of others but there is no clue as to who they might be.

It is now believed that at some point he lived with an Essene community. The Essenes, said by some to be a break-away group from Zadokite priests[17] were a Jewish sect which flourished from the 2nd century BC to the 1st AD. A smaller sect than those of the Pharisees and Sadducees, the Essenes were a puritan group, dedicated to an ascetic life rather like that of Celtic monasteries, embracing poverty and daily immersion. They lived in communes in various cities. It has been suggested that Jesus and his disciples celebrated his last Passover meal at an Essene house on Mount Zion. To them, temple worship and those who led it were completely corrupt; it was rejected by them as was the Day of the Passover, which they moved to the previous Tuesday. Their most famous community was that at Qumran, where the Dead Sea Scrolls were discovered in 1947. The ruins of the community buildings have been uncovered at an inhospitable site In the Judean desert, not far from the Dead Sea. This is generally believed to be the place to which John retreated and from where he came to the River Jordan to begin his ministry. John's ministry certainly gives some signs of his possible links with them. He came out of the desert, dressed as an ascetic and lived on wild beans called locusts [I was given a pod once in Palestine] and wild honey. His message proclaimed the approach of the Day of the Lord, with the coming soon of the Messiah. The people needed to be warned of the divine wrath which was to come soon, with its attendant need for the people to repent and be baptised in the Jordan as a ritual sign of their being cleansed from their sins.

Jesus came and joined the queue of those seeking this baptism of repentance. This he did, not for his own sake, but to stand with those who needed to do so and to represent all who would not or could not come. Jesus' action was vicarious for the sake of all humanity.

John's verbal lashing of the crowds and his attacks on the "brood of vipers" of the religious establishment certainly concurred with Essene thinking. The Baptist paid the price usually demanded of anyone who disturbed the established order as he did. He was arrested where he remained until his execution. He had assumed that the One who was to follow would have a similar message. In prison he heard reports of his cousin's ministry and sent his followers to ask '"Are you the one who is to come, or are we to wait for another?" Jesus answered them, "Go and tell John what you hear and see: the blind receive their sight, the lame walk, the lepers are cleansed, the deaf hear, the dead are raised and the poor have good news brought to them. And blessed is anyone who takes no offence in me."[18] Jesus takes advantage of the question asked by the Baptist's followers, with the crowd listening, to set out once more his manifesto for the Kingdom. He then speaks of John, ascetic and prophets, calling him the messenger of God sent to prepare the way, a quotation from Malachi 3.1 (the Greek word used here is *angelos-angel)* and the prophet Elijah (Malachi 4.5).

Lord, you sent John the Baptist to call your children back to yourself. In our day you call us to bear our witness to you. May your Spirit so guide us that by our deeds, words and attitudes and by the manner of our living together as your people, we may be heralds of your coming; through Jesus Christ our Saviour.

Questions for thought or discussion

1. Does the Baptist's kind of life-style have a place in the Church today?
2. Have the churches always chosen the teachings of Jesus rather than those of John the Baptist?
3. Where is the redeeming work of Christ to be seen today?
4. What is our role?

Chapter Four

Mary's Visitor

The Lord himself shall give you a sign: Behold, a virgin shall conceive, and bear a son, and shall call his name Immanuel. (Isaiah 7.14)

There are two churches at Nazareth which claim to be the site of the meeting of Mary with the angel. One is the Orthodox Church of St. Gabriel, built in 1769 over a fresh-water spring, the town's only water supply for many centuries. The other is the Catholic Basilica of the Annunciation, built between 1955 and 1969 over the site of an early fifth century Byzantine church and replacing the 17th century Franciscan church which collapsed in 1955. This beautiful edifice is the largest church built in the Holy Land during the last eight hundred years and is reputed to stand above Mary's home.

Which is correct? Luke's Gospel offers no clue. The local tradition finds no problem in this. A well-brought-up girl like Mary would be horrified if a man approached her in a public place and she would run home at top speed. This tradition is found too in the second century *Protoevangelium of James*, which says this: 'And Mary took the pitcher and went forth to draw water, and behold a voice said, "Hail, thou who art highly favoured among women." And she looked on the right and on the left to see whence this voice came. And trembling she went to her house and put down the pitcher, and took the purple and sat down on her seat and drew out the thread. And behold an angel of the Lord suddenly stood before her and said, "Do not fear, Mary, for you have found grace before the Lord of all things and shall conceive of his Word."' (11.1-2). Nazareth Christians are happy with this apocryphal explanation.

Luke may not speak of the place but he does describe the event, dating it as in the sixth month of Elizabeth's pregnancy, and declaring that the angel Gabriel [Hero of God] came and greeted Mary. The King James Bible translates as, "Hail, thou that art highly favoured" and most English translations since then, including the *Jerusalem Bible*, have used similar words. The *Hail Mary* with its "Full of grace" comes from the earlier Latin Vulgate translation.

The King James Bible tells us that Mary "was troubled at this saying." Other translations use stronger phrases like "greatly troubled, deeply perturbed, much perplexed, deeply disturbed," all of which reflect Luke's Greek and, if anything, these may well be understating her panic. How can she be "the favoured of God" when she is such a nobody? How can she, who is one of the poor of the land and living in a real backwater, be "blessed among women?" Obviously, these words would trouble her greatly for she does not count, a young woman, powerless in a male society, but the angel tells her not to be afraid. Gabriel's response overcomes her fear by telling her that God has a task for her and that the "Holy Spirit will come upon" her, a phrase used by Luke on eight occasions in his two New Testament books, including his description of the Holy Spirit coming upon the disciples on the day of Pentecost.[19] Her son "will be holy and called the Son of God." She is to bear the promised "Son of David", the Messiah. Such talk must have left young Mary more fearful and dumbfounded but, so as to overcome her doubts and fears, Mary is given a sign: her cousin, the elderly and barren Elizabeth, is pregnant. At once, Mary's deep faith is restored and she responds: "Behold, I am the handmaid of the Lord, let it be to me according to your word."

Gabriel's message is life-changing for Mary and history-changing for the world. The Lord had chosen her for a particular role in his plan of salvation. She is not promised the happiness most of us seek; rather she is being called to a task which will be for her a source of particular blessing. This betrothed girl is to go through the pains of child birth outside marriage, with the consequent shame to herself and her family of bearing a child outside wedlock. She cannot know how either Joseph or her family will respond but there can be no doubt about the response of her community.

However, her blessing will be found in the child she is to bear. He will be called *Jesus*: this is the Greek version of the Hebrew *Joshua* or, in its fuller form, *Yehoshuah (God is salvation* or *God saves)*. He is also to be called "the Son of the Most High and will be given the throne of his father David." Her baby is the Promised Messiah. It is in Exodus 4.22 that the Old Testament for the first time speaks of God as the Father and Israel as his son – 'thus says the Lord: "Let my son go that he may worship me" (see also Hosea 11.1 and Jeremiah 31.20). With the establishment of the Jewish Kingdom it is the king who comes to embody this sonship. So Psalm 2.7 declares, 'he said to me, "You are my Son; today I have begotten you."' (See 2 Samuel 7.14). By the time of the Annunciation Israel was waiting for the coming of the promised Lord's Anointed, "King David's greater Son." Expectation filled the air.

Mary has only one question – How? She is told that "the Holy Spirit will come upon her." This book is not a place for theological debate. For those who accept the doctrine of the Virgin Birth there is no problem here. For those who cannot accept this as a biological fact, it is worth remembering the comment of George B. Caird in his Pelican commentary that it was by a creative act of the Holy Spirit that Jesus entered his Sonship, the Spirit who acted at the creation. The important declaration here is theological, that God comes into human life in Jesus Christ. The questioning in Luke's day was not as to the divinity of Jesus but as to his humanity. It is suggested that the heretical teachers to whom Luke refers in Acts 20.28-30 were Docetists, who denied his humanity. Then, in the Old Testament, the phrase "virgin daughter" is used to describe nations and cities but usually with special reference to Israel. Nations such as Egypt (Jeremiah 46.11), Sidon (Isaiah 23.12) and Babylon (Isaiah 47.1). The "virgin daughter" describes Jerusalem/Zion (2 Kings 19.21; Isaiah 37.22; Lamentation 2.11). In Jeremiah 14.17 it is applied to "my people," and Lamentation 1.15 uses it for Judah. Two of the prophets use the phrase "the virgin of Israel" to speak of the people's loss of purity and its restoration. So, in declaiming the apostasy of the nation, Amos 5.2 declares that "The virgin of Israel is fallen; she is forsaken on her land; there is none to lift her up." Jeremiah uses the name twice: in 18.13 "Therefore, now among the heathen, who hath heard such things: the virgin of Israel hath done a very terrible thing," but the prophet too speaks of restoration: verse 4: Again, I will build thee. O virgin of Israel: thou shalt be adorned with thy tabrets, and shalt go forth in the dances of them that make merry," whilst verse 21 sings, "O virgin of Israel, turn again to these thy cities."

Mary is chosen for this task by God himself; in this way she will be "his favoured one" as the angel promised. She is reminded that "with God nothing is impossible." That is enough for her! Though, like Abraham, the father of her people, she must go, not knowing where. Probably, Mary's head had been full of plans for her marriage, just as Joseph too would have plans, but both are challenged by God's plans for them and the world. That goes for us too. Her response is total, as is that of Joseph! "Behold the handmaid of the Lord!"

Lord God, you called Mary to be your servant and gave her grace to be the bearer of the Christ Child. Give us the same grace that we, in our turn, may be bearers of Christ to every corner of our lives.

Questions for thought or discussion

1. What does it mean for us to have the Lord's favour?

2. Mary rejoices in being given a part to play in the event which declares the coming of God's Kingdom. Her saying YES in faith to God's call involves the becoming the mother of Jesus. How are we to say YES?

3. Read the Magnificat. Mary sings of a world turned upside down. Is that our song too? What does that involve practically?

4. Mary's song comes from deep within a people's longing and hope and provides her with an answer. Does it do so for us?

Chapter Five

Family Get-Together

And you shall rejoice before the Lord your God, you together
with your sons, and your daughters, your male and female
slaves, and the Levites who reside in your town
(Deuteronomy 12.12)

Sometime after the angel's visit, Mary leaves home quickly in
order to travel to a town in Judaea, believed to be Ein Karem,
a distance of some eighty or so miles and a journey of several
days. Western Churches observe the Visitation on 31st May, an
adjustment from the 2nd July of the Julian calendar. She would
have walked or ridden on a donkey but why, in her condition,
did she risk the journey and why depart in such a rush? Mary
may have wished to share her cousin's joy or to tell her own
story to a sympathetic ear or to have confirmation of what had
been told her. But it would not be the first time or the last for an
unmarried pregnant girl to be packed off to the country to bear
her child out of sight and criticism, so as to hide her parents'
shame. It could be too that being in her Nazareth home with her
parents and family was too uncomfortable for her. Maybe she is
running away from Joseph. Whatever the reason, she undertakes
the journey. On arrival at the priest's house, she enters in and
greets her cousin. Luke says that the first response to her voice
comes not from the other mother-to-be but from the boy in
Elizabeth's womb, who jumps.

Elizabeth is filled with the Holy Spirit, a rare event for the
women of the New Testament and she tells her cousin that her
baby jumped for joy in the womb on hearing Mary's voice.
Elizabeth greets her cousin in words which she would not have

thought suitable for an unmarried, pregnant girl. "Blessed are you among women and blessed is the fruit of your womb... And blessed is she who believed that there would be a fulfilment of what was spoken to her by the Lord." Just as the first words of the *Ave Maria* come from the Angel's greeting to Mary, so the second sentence is taken from Elizabeth's words. This greeting must have come as a great comfort to Elizabeth's cousin in view of her physical and social condition.

Mary speaks or sings in response the words now called the Magnificat, the first word of the Latin version. The Magnificat is to be heard every day in many languages in churches around the world.

Mary's song bears close resemblance to that of Hannah in 1 Samuel 2.1-10, the outburst of praise from a woman whose long period of barrenness is ended by God's response to her prayer. In many of the Psalms the author moves from personal concerns to those of God's People. So, here Mary, after singing of her own being lifted from lowliness to this blessedness, goes on to speak of God's concern for the poor and downtrodden. Though Mary uses the past tense, she is looking forward just as the prophets did when they used the prophetic perfect: if God has promised it, it is as good as done! In the promise of the coming of his Son, God has acted and it will come to pass. Mary's people had lived under foreign rule for centuries and only collaborators found wealth. "The poor of the land" were seen to be those humble, simple trusting folk like Mary and Joseph, Elizabeth and Zechariah, shepherds and foreigners, Simeon and Anna in the Temple. Mary's Son will bring God's will to pass but he will cast down every barrier and fill every chasm between peoples in his message of forgiveness, healing and reconciliation for all. When this happens, pride will be replaced by humility, the sense of status will disappear whilst no one will have too little and no one will seek too much. In this way, the promises of God to Abraham and his descendants will be realised, "in you shall all the families of earth be blessed" are fulfilled (Genesis 12.3).

Mary remains in her cousin's home for three months. Why did she stay? Perhaps it was to support Elizabeth to the end of her pregnancy; perhaps because she has nowhere else to go, or a mixture of both reasons. But then she does return. No explanation is offered but it may well be that Joseph, after his vision, comes to fetch her and begin the process of restoring to her home town and to respectability.

Holy Father, you call us to live as your children, sisters and brothers together, through the self-giving of your Son, Jesus Christ our Brother. Guide each and all of us by your Holy Spirit that, by the way Christians live together in love and harmony, the world may come to know and love you; through the same, Jesus Christ our Lord.

Questions for thought or discussion

1. Is the Church meant to be our new family? If so, what does that mean in practice?
2. How do you/your church treat people in the congregation who are not quite the same as us?
3. Friends appreciate families with an open-door policy. Can you apply that to your church and your own attitudes?

Chapter Six

Joseph the Carpenter

Lord, who may abide in thy tabernacle? Who may dwell in thy holy hill? He who walks uprightly, and works righteousness, and speaks the truth in his heart.
(Psalm 15)

I have always felt sorry for Joseph. It seems to me that he has had a raw deal from history and tradition. It came home to me on my first visit to a Roman Catholic Church, decades ago. The priest pointed to the statue of Mary and spoke of her importance and then turned to Joseph saying "I am not sure why he is here. Perhaps it is just to keep the balance." And is that all? Surely, if Mary is the epitome of all that is good in womanhood and motherhood, then is not Joseph, by the same token, the symbol of what is good in manhood and fatherhood?

Both Luke and Matthew tell us that Joseph and Mary are betrothed. This is far more than Western engagements. Betrothal involved a legal contract involving not only the individuals concerned but also their families. The couple was as good as married, totally reserved for each other. When the woman actually became a wife, then she went to live in her husband's house, often the home of his extended family, and the marriage was consummated.

Matthew tells us that Joseph discovers that his betrothed is pregnant. Others must know too, including her family. If it is still a secret, then it will not be long before tongues begin to wag in this small town, especially as Mary has always given the impression of being a 'good girl.' How did Joseph find out? Did Mary tell him? Was it her family or did he hear the neighbour's gossip? Even to a pious man, her story would seem far-fetched.

Poor Joseph is dishonoured, both by his bride's condition and by the gossip that will fly around the town. What can he do? Betrothal was legally binding and under Jewish Law it could only be put aside in one of two ways. He can go to court and have the shame removed from his shoulders to those of her family, who will also pay the costs. In the good old days, before the Romans took over, righteous men would have stoned her to death, as the Law demanded. Now they can only cast their words at her but their hateful cries too will be cruel. The alternative is that he sets the betrothal aside privately in the presence of two witnesses. The family can say little in these circumstances and she will be cast off in disgrace. The King James Bible says that Joseph is "a just man", otherwise described as "a good man, a man of principle, a man of honour, a man who always did what was right." That is, he was a good, straight-as-die man and what one would expect of an upright Pharisee, who kept the Law but, unlike many of his contemporaries, his piety was mixed with compassion. He makes no excuses for her nor does he condemn her as he ends their bond. It is easy to imagine something of his pain, anguish and inner turmoil as he prepares to do so.

Then he too gets a visit from "an angel of the Lord", who comes on this occasion during the night. The conversation is revealing. The angel offers no words of comfort, sympathy or understanding, the things most people expect from their faith. Instead, Gabriel brings reassurance and marching orders. Joseph is to take Mary to his home as his wife, for it is by the Holy Spirit that she has conceived. Her child is to be raised as his. Under Jewish Law, adoption conferred the same status as kinship.

What is Joseph being told here? He is being told that Mary is his and yet not his. This is, of course, true of every human relationship, a fact which is easily forgotten or set aside. No one of us is the property of any other human being. True human relationship is based on a voluntary sharing of what we are. There is that which belongs only to self, that which is shared and that which belongs to God. For Mary at this time, God's call has a prior demand on her. That is hard for her and hard for Joseph and it is true for us all. Whatever Joseph's feelings he will serve God. That is the way by which the world will be saved. Joseph is hearing too that the Child is not his and yet is his. The child is God's and God's gift to him. Joseph is to adopt the child as his own. He is to carry the burden of fatherhood. Many will see this baby as Joseph's disgrace and folly. Fingers will point and tongues will wag. People will turn their backs and smile mockingly. But Joseph is to accept this child who has brought him so much pain, even before he is born. Karl Barth suggests that Joseph has a passive role but this is an active passivity, just like Mary's.

Joseph will go ahead with the marriage. When the time comes for his visit to Bethlehem, he will take Mary with him. It is only the men who had to register. Why the folly of taking a very pregnant woman on a journey of almost a hundred miles in winter (there was heavy snow in Jerusalem and Bethlehem in early December 2013), either on foot or on a donkey's back? Why not leave her with her own family or with his relatives? This is not a family outing for the sake of reunion but imposed by Rome and therefore not a happy trip. So why take her? Is it that he is afraid to leave her alone in Nazareth? How would the neighbours, who later tried to throw the man Jesus over a cliff, react? What might his offended relatives or her disgraced family react in his absence? Whatever the explanation, Joseph does not leave her there to face the birth alone in such a hateful atmosphere. He takes her with him to Bethlehem and in doing so he declares that they belong together because of their betrothal but more, because they are now bound together by the call of God.

In the story of the birth and childhood of Jesus, the loving obedience of Joseph has a special place. Jesus becomes the son of Joseph by official or unofficial adoption but this is a two-way adoption, for Joseph too is adopted as father. He takes up the responsibility and authority of fatherhood. It is he who names the child. That is the father's prerogative, even though Joseph has been told beforehand what the boy is to be called. The child Jesus must respect and obey him just as any child must. Jesus becomes one of us.

So Joseph is to guard holy things or, rather, this holy life, through which God's own life will be released into the world. Joseph's role may appear to be less than that of Mary and it may be of lesser duration because, as the carol says, "Joseph was an old man." Nonetheless, it has an essential place in the story of the incarnation of the Lord. The Orthodox Church calls Mary Theotokos or God-Bearer. She carries Jesus in her womb for nine months and then in her arms. Finally, in her love, she nurses his dead body. But, does not Joseph have a similar role? Is he not a God-Enabler? This couple are the first members of the New Humanity, the first of us. The initiative is always God's, who releases life into the world via an empty womb and empty tomb. Christmas and Easter are part of one action. A new relationship is created between God and humanity and there is hope for the world. But this divine initiative always seeks human response in trust, acceptance and loving obedience. That is so for Mary and Joseph. They must learn through doing it what it means to die to self, as parents always must. Joseph and Mary are faithful in their task because first they see and hear God – the Emmanuel, who is here and now.

Lord God, you called Joseph the Carpenter to play his part in the story of the world's salvation, giving him the gifts he needed to help bring up the boy Jesus in the way he should go. Fill us too with grace, humility and righteousness that we too may play our part in the coming of Christ into our world and our generation.

Questions for thought or discussion

1. What is the role of Joseph? What does he have to tell us?

2. "It is Joseph's turn to come to central stage and, in these verses, we remember the way in which, through God's power, he was able to turn a potential ruin into love; to transform disgrace into grace, thus enabling life to flourish." (Archdeacon Andrew Jones). What opportunities are given to us Christians and as churches to pull those in need from the ruins of life and offer them grace?

3. Are we also called to be a sort of Christ-bearers and Christ-bearers, the means by which Christ is born into the world in our generation and every situation?

Chapter Seven

City of David

But you, Bethlehem Ephrathah, though you are little among the thousands of Judah, yet out of you shall come forth to me the One to be ruler in Israel, whose goings forth have been from of old, from everlasting.
(Micah 5.2)

Luke reports that the birth of Jesus took place at Bethlehem in the reign of Octavian, known as Caesar Augustus (23 BC-14 AD). Born in 63 BC, Gaius Octavius was the great-nephew of Julius Caesar by marriage. After Caesar's murder, his will was read, in which Caesar made him his heir. He then changed his name to Gaius Julius Caesar Octavianus. He and Mark Antony executed 300 senators and 2000 knights before defeating the forces of Brutus. Mark Antony fell under the spell of Cleopatra, Queen of Egypt, and he broke with Octavian, divorcing his daughter Octavia. War ensued and ended with the suicide of Antony and Cleopatra and the adding of Egypt to the Roman Empire. Octavian was given the name Augustus by the Roman Senate in 27 BC. He observed the forms of republican government but became the world's most powerful man, and as Pontifex Maximus, Rome's high priest, he was both the spiritual and secular ruler. He was deified by the Senate after his death in 14 AD. Later, at the Graeco-Roman city of Halicarnassus in Asia Minor, an inscription was set up which described him as "saviour of the whole world." According to John Buchan's description of the funeral of Augustus, "Men comforted themselves, reflecting that Augustus was a god and gods do not die"[20] but die he did. Augustus arranged for his stepson and son-in-law Tiberius to become co-regent, becoming regent when the former died.

Luke points out that this Caesar Augustus, pagan ruler of the world, became God's instrument just like the Persian Ruler Cyrus (Isaiah 45.1, who freed the Israelites from their Babylonian captivity). Augustus, by calling the census, is given a part to play in the coming of a ruler, whose kingdom's boundaries would extend far beyond the frontiers of his great empire.

The city of Rome was a by-word for wealth, power and authority as well as intrigue, corruption and vice. Its soldiers, civil servants and workers were drawn from the ranks of its conquered peoples, whilst its citizens called only for "bread and circuses." Theodore Mommsen (1817-1903), the great historian of Rome wrote "the world was old and not even Caesar could make it young again." Such periods arise from time to time in world history.

Bethlehem, on the other hand, was a small town, some six miles from Jerusalem. However, its significance lay in its history. The earliest historical reference comes from the 14th century BC, in a letter from Abdu-Heba, prince of Jerusalem, who complains that "Bit-Lahmi had gone over to the Apiru." Its first biblical appearance is in Genesis 35.19: "So Rachel died, and she was buried on the way to Ephrath (that is Bethlehem)..." The tomb is still there and in happier days it was visited by women, Jewish, Christian and Muslim, unable to have children. There are other references, including most of the book of Ruth but its main importance in the Old Testament is based on its association with King David. This was a royal town.

What evidence is there for the census mentioned by Luke? Periodic censuses for the purpose of tax gathering and military conscription were introduced into Egypt in the second millennium BC. There exists a papyrus document, written in Greek, which shows that such censuses did take place. A papyrus document[21] dated AD.104 exists, which contains an order from Gaius Vibius Maximus, Prefect/Governor of Egypt between AD 103-107, for all those living in the area ruled by him to return to their own homes to register themselves (*apographēs*) in a census before one Festus, a cavalry commander, who will then issue the signatories with documents of proof. Usually it was the eldest male in a family who provided details of the property and all residents therein, including family members, employees, lodgers and slaves. Each person's name, age and relationship with the head of the household were required. The earliest census took place in Gaul in BC 27 and resulted in riots and resistance.

This census is dated by Luke as "When Quirinius was governor of Syria." We know that Publius Sulpicius Qurinius, member of a Roman aristocratic family (BC 51-AD 21) was appointed legate/ governor of the province of Syria (Samaria, Judea and Idumea) in AD 6, after the banishment of Herod Archelaus, tetrarch of Judea. He returned to Rome six years later and became close to the emperor Tiberius until his death nine years later, when he was honoured with a public funeral. According to the Jewish historian Josephus,

> Cyrenius, a Roman senator, and one who had gone through other magistracies, till he had been consul, and one who, on other accounts, was of great dignity, came at this time into Syria, with a few others, being sent by Caesar to be a judge of that nation, and to take an account of their substance. Coponius also, a man of the equestrian order, was sent together with him, to have the supreme power over the Jews. Moreover, Cyrenius came himself into Judea, which was now added to the province of Syria, to take an account of their substance, and to dispose of Archelaus's money.

Josephus sees this census as a factor in the rising against Roman rule led by Judas of Galilee,[22] who declared that the census and its resulting taxation were a form of slavery. Though this uprising was crushed, Josephus saw this movement as developing into the Zealots of Jesus' day.

As has been noted, it is hard to see why Mary accompanied Joseph on this arduous journey, unless there would be danger in leaving her at Nazareth. So Mary goes with him. They go to Bethlehem (The House of Bread), set in a fairly fertile region, with the wilderness of Sinai to the south and the desert leading down to the Dead Sea and the Jordan Valley and then the Mountains of Moab to the east. This is the place from which shall come God's "Living Bread."

Joseph and Mary arrived at Bethlehem at a very busy time for the town, which was crowded. Luke tells us that there was no room at the inn. The town was crowded with visitors who had every right to be there. Perhaps they had made reservations or were regular guests. Maybe it just happened that way: "First come, first served" or "the devil take the hindmost." That's fair enough. They might have had the latest chariots or the fastest horses that money could be. They were not encumbered with a pregnant girl. Someone always has to be last. It is usually the poor.

But what of family? Both Joseph and Mary were descendants of David and, surely, there must have been relatives of some sort in the town. Was every house so absolutely crowded that the laws of hospitality could not be observed, especially for a woman in Mary's condition? My brother-in-law, when in the sixth form, was invited to spend a weekend in London by a Jewish friend. When he asked where they were to stay, he was startled by the reply, "I don't know yet." On arrival in the metropolis, they went to street of large houses in north London, where the friend knew no one. After examining carefully those residences with scrolls on their door posts, the friend said, "This will do." He knocked a door and announced whose son he was and they were honoured guests for three nights.

Luke's account raises many questions about our traditional interpretations. Our Nativity plays have led us to think that Mary gave birth immediately upon their arrival in town but

Luke lacks this sense of immediacy. He writes, "While they were there the time came for her to deliver her child." Then where did this happen? Did Joseph go from one family residence to another, knocking the door and being turned away? If so, why were these Bethlehem doors closed? Were these houses already filled by other relatives who could travel faster than this pregnant woman? Had the news of family disgrace already arrived from Nazareth? Could it have been that it was then that the couple turned to the inns, only to hear "Full up!" at every door? The Greek word *kataluma* generally translated here as "inn" also means "guest room." The same word appears in Luke 22.11: "The teacher asks you, 'where is the guest room, where I may eat the Passover with my disciples?" (NRSV). The other reference to an inn comes in the Parable of the Good Samaritan, Luke 10.34: "Then he put him on his own animal, brought him to an inn, and took care of him." Here the word inn translates the Greek *pandocheion*. Some scholars argue that Mary would never have given birth to her son at an inn, because they were such dreadful places but it could be argued that they would be just right for that very reason.

But even today many Palestinian families live in houses of one room, with no extra space for children, let alone guests. It was commonplace in the past, including Britain in the Middle Ages for families and their animals to live under the same roof, the latter providing warmth for the family, whilst the family knew that their animals were safe from thieves.

How do dictionaries translate *kataluma*? Both The abridged version of the [Classical Greek] *Lexicon of Liddell and Scott (1949 impression)* and Alexander Souter's *A Pocket Lexicon to the Greek New Testament (1949)* use the same words: "an inn, lodging." I turned to my computer for more modern works and discovered a similarity: *The New American Standard Greek Lexicon* translates thus: (1) inn, lodging place (2) eating room, dining room. The word *kataluma* appears in several places in Greek versions of the Hebrew Scriptures. One English translation of Jeremiah 41.8 reads: "Lord, hope of Israel, you save in time of evil; why do you become as an alien upon the land and a local neighbour turning aside for a guest room." This suggests that God cannot find a welcome among his people but "turns aside" in a guest room as a paying guest. Kinship and solidarity are absent and the *kataluma* becomes the symbol of estrangement.

That comment underlines the tragedy of the "no room at the inn or in a guest room" in the Nativity story. The word is also used by Mark and Luke to describe the Upper Room where Jesus spent his last evening with his disciples. Many commentators use the Upper Room's *kataluma* as a means of rejecting the use of "inn" in the birth account, seeing an unfortunate lack of space for as the reason for the failure of Joseph and Mary to find a bed. But, equally, if *kataluma* suggests rejection at Bethlehem, it can have the same message in the Upper Room story. The Upper Room is a *kataluma*, to which turns as he is being rejected. Jesus finds shelter with the Essenes, the puritan sect outside the main stream of Israel. It is here that Jesus, the object of hostility and rejection celebrates the Passover with his disciples on the night before his crucifixion. Then they too must walk the way of the Cross.

Clearly there is no room in either house or inn. The child must be born elsewhere. Then a more compassionate inn-keeper took pity on them and offered a different place (probably, at a price); tradition has said that this was a stable. Where else would one find a manger (or stall)? Luke makes no reference to animals; "ox and ass" first appear in apocryphal gospels based on the words of Isaiah 1. 3: "The ox knows his master and the donkey his master's crib; but Israel does not know, my people do not understand." The belief that this was a cave is first recorded by Justin (c. A.D. 150). Properties were built above caves, as the traditional site of Nazareth reveals. The present chapel of the Nativity at Bethlehem is but part of a whole series of caves and passageways: at noon each day a Catholic procession goes down steps at St. Catherine's church, each person with a light and a Latin prayer book, and proceeds along such a series, singing psalms, a memorable experience for the author in 1989.

But what if the householder had known who they were? – would he not have turned out the occupants of the guest room? Or what about the innkeeper? What if he had known who this girl's child was? He would have found space, even by turning someone out to do so. A "by-appointment" shield above the door would have been good for business. The town council would have erected a plaque but no one knew, no one was meant to know. All they saw was an unmarried girl, about to give birth to a peasant boy, and accompanied by an old man who should have known better. Feckless people like them could be a burden on the community and deserved no help.

The gospel accounts make no mention of a cave or even a stable, only a manger. The earliest references to a cave are found in the writings of Justin Martyr (c.100-165), who in his *Dialogue with Trypho*, circa 150, declares that the Saviour was born in a cave near the village of Bethlehem. Such cave-stables were far from uncommon in this area The *Protoevangelium of James*, an apocryphal work from the second century says this:

And they came into the middle of the road, and Mary said to him: Take me down from off the [donkey], for that which is in me presses to come forth. And he took her down from off the [donkey], and said to her: Where shall I lead you, and cover your disgrace? For the place is desert. And he found a cave there, and led her into it; and leaving his two sons beside her, he went out to seek a midwife in the district of Bethlehem...

The New Testament accounts make no mention of a midwife. In them the only person mentioned as being with Mary is Joseph. Is it the disgrace of unmarried pregnancy which means that

47

she must face giving birth, not only without the aids of modern medicine and nursing but also without a clean bed, the aid of other women and the absence of her mother?

In this stable cave, Mary gives birth to her son, her first born "and wraps him in swaddling clothes." Swaddling was an ancient and fairly universal custom, certainly practised in Europe until the seventeenth century. Infants were wrapped tightly in strips of cloth so that they would be kept warm and their limbs would grow straight but actually this caused major restriction.

It is said that on the site of the inn, early Christians had built a small church. This was destroyed by the Emperor Tiberius, who built on the same spot a temple to Adonis, so as to destroy any memory of this Jesus. When Helena visited Bethlehem and asked where the Saviour was born, she was shown the temple. She and Constantine commissioned the basilica in 327 and it was dedicated by Helena on 31 May 339, only to be destroyed by fire in 530 during the Samaritan revolt against Rome. The present church was built on the same site in 565 by the Emperor Justinian. Interior steps lead down to a cave, said to be the place of the birth. This is one of a whole series of caves linked together by passageways.

Jerome, translator of the Bible's Hebrew and Greek texts in Latin (the Vulgate), wrote his Epistle 58 (AD 395):

From Hadrian's time [C2nd AD] until the reign of Constantine, for about 180 years... Bethlehem, now ours, and the earth's most sacred spot... was overshadowed by a grove of Thammuz, which is Adonis, and in the cave where the infant Messiah once cried, the paramour of Venus was bewailed.

The place of Jesus' birth was, of course, far removed from our Christmas card scenes and certainly lacking in modern standards of hygiene. It was a working stable, with all its associated sounds and smells and lacking in comfort even by the standards of the day, though the presence of the animals would have provided some warmth.

The circumstances of this birth have little in comparison with royal births, even at this time but can be compared with refugee births. Unlike almost all of those of royal birth are forgotten; this birth is remembered around the world with joy and thanksgiving.

With the poor and mean and lowly lived on earth our Saviour holy.

God our Father, you sent your Son to be born as Prince of Peace at Bethlehem. We pray for the people of Bethlehem and all the Holy Land and all who live in places of fear and conflict. May your Spirit bring justice, reconciliation and peace within and between the nations, within your Church and in our hearts; through Jesus Christ our Saviour

Questions for thought or discussion

1. What is the significance of Bethlehem in the story of the Nativity?
2. Do you believe that Christmas is not just back there but a reality today? How do you show it?
3. How do you know that Christ is born in you and in your church?

Chapter Eight

A Common Lot

The humble also shall increase their joy in the Lord, and the poor among men shall rejoice in the Holy One of Israel. (Isaiah 29.19)

The inn is full and the town is crowded but below the town there is plenty of empty space. The only people down there are shepherds and they do not count. The people in the town know that and so do the shepherds themselves. The shepherds are down there, "keeping watch over their flocks by night," except that they are not their flocks. They care for the sheep of the people in the town and in the villages around, who can afford not to do this despised work themselves. Who wants to go and be with them? They are neither respectable nor acceptable.

Their work means that they are unable to observe all the minutiae of religious observance, like washing their hands with ritual regularity. So they are barred from religious circles and decent society. What are they like, these shepherds? What do we know of their characters and personalities? Are they nice men or are they no-good scoundrels? We do not know. Is there any faith among them? Do they know and trust that the Lord is their Shepherd and that he will have more understanding and compassion for them than his rather superior servants? We are not told, but they and everyone else would find that hard to believe for these men, are the poor of the land.

William Barclay points out that the Temple flocks were pastured near Bethlehem and wonders whether these men were special shepherds keeping watch over special sheep.[23] He calls this "a lovely thought." Surely, the point of Luke's story is these are ordinary, common keepers of sheep, representing the ordinary poor of the world.

Then, as they mind their own business, suddenly they have a visitor who brings them a message – Good News for all the world! And they are the first to hear this "Good News for the Poor." They are told of a new-born boy, who is Saviour, Messiah (Christ) and Lord. The Jews never referred to the Messiah as "Lord," that title being reserved for God alone. They spoke only of "the Lord's Messiah" and used in reference to Simeon, to whom "it had been revealed ... by the Holy Spirit that he would not see death before he had seen the Lord's Messiah."[24]

He comes to people longing for liberation – to the Jews weary of their conquerors and the sins which caused their downfall. The news is for the Gentile world also seeking salvation. The gods of Greece and Rome seemed inadequate and too much like human beings. Some gentiles turned to Isis of Egypt and others to Asclepius, the healing god of Asia Minor, whilst some were attracted by the Yahweh of the Jews, a clean and moral deity. There were many too who turned to worshipping Caesar, the architect of the empire's Pax Romana and of Rome's prosperity. However, real hunger was not satisfied by any of these. These nobodies see the heavens light up with the glory of God and they are told of a birth. It is for them and their sort in particular. There is a new-born boy, who is Saviour, Messiah (Christ) and Lord. Pagan gods were often called 'saviour' but Isaiah speaks in this way of God himself.[25] Luke limits the use of "saviour" to Jesus,[26] whilst neither Matthew nor Mark uses the word at all. His coming is to people longing for liberation – to the Jews weary of their conquerors and the sins which caused their downfall. The shepherds learn that they are among that number. God's peace is being poured out on human beings. Later, when speaking of the baptism of Jesus, Luke (3.22) will present Jesus as the representative human being. The shepherds are told that true peace can come only when God's Kingdom is established. Then they are given a sign to confirm the promise: "you will find a child wrapped in bands of cloth and lying in a manger." There have already been two such signs: Zechariah's being struck deaf and dumb and Elizabeth's pregnancy.

Then they hear the music, which only they can hear. In normal circumstances, at a village birth, the local musicians would serenade the mother and child but there are none at the stable door. Instead, a heavenly choir appears, "a multitude of the heavenly host." The scene is reminiscent of Isaiah's vision in the Temple, where the Lord of Hosts is praised by the seraphim and then the prophet is told to go and tell the people what he has seen and heard.

In the Old Testament, the God of Israel is often called "the Lord of Hosts"[27] to express his majesty and sovereign power. 'Hosts' comes from military usage, where it meant an army.[28] Then it was extended to any term of hard service.[29] In the Book of Numbers it appears several times to designate the Temple service of the Levites.[30] Ancient thinkers saw the stars as a kind of military force, "the hosts of heaven," reflecting the glory of the "Lord of hosts." This was particularly so in the cultures of Assyria and Babylon which had a great influence on Israel. Frequent warnings appear in the Scriptures against such ideas, beginning with Deuteronomy 4.19: "when you look up to the heavens and see the sun and moon and stars, all the host of heaven, do not be led astray and bow down and worship them..." Israel took the Babylonian concept of divine assemblies and conceived of the Lord presiding over his heavenly council. So the prophet Micaiah tells King Jehosophat that he "saw the Lord sitting on his throne, with all the host of heaven standing beside him to the right and to the left."[31] Sometimes the two ideas merge as in Job 37. 4.7: "Where were you when I laid the foundation of the earth... when the morning stars sang together and all the heavenly beings shouted for joy?"

This choir now sings to celebrate the new creation, being brought about in the birth of this child. Its messianic statement is: "Glory to God in the highest and peace on earth and among those whom he favours." Its opening words will be repeated on Palm Sunday when the Saviour Messiah enters Jerusalem on his way to his cross.[32] The choir sings, "Peace on earth for those to whom God favours;" James Moffatt translates the phrase as "men of God's good pleasure."[33] The shepherds hear of this gift of peace for them, the forerunners of the common folk who will hear him gladly!

The vision departs and the shepherds act on what they have seen and heard and hurry up the hill to Bethlehem. They take a risk and leave their sheep to find their Shepherd. They find the place and there is no palace, no courtiers, and no guards. All they see is a child in a manger, with his unmarried mother and an old man, with the animals. Isaiah 1.3 had said that "the ox knows its owner, and the donkey its master's crib; but Israel does not know, my people do not understand." It is likely that the shepherds were ignorant of these words but now they see that this baby is just like them, in their world. They see for themselves what they heard earlier. God has come – to them! They recognise God, in their own world. He has come to them, loving, forgiving, caring, healing, reconciling, redeeming.

The shepherds turn to go, taking their excitement with them. The cave is silent again. Mary is left with her thoughts, treasuring them in her heart and pondering the significance of what is happening. She has been the victim of scandal, sorrow and pain but the object of disgrace has become the vehicle of grace. She does not understand but she accepts and obeys. She is the Christ-bearer, the prototype of the new humanity. Joseph is not mentioned in the account of the shepherds' visit but he must be there somewhere, or on an errand. He has been deeply hurt by Mary's pregnancy. First, he thought that his trust had been abused. Then his good name suffered as the neighbours sniggered – "No fool like an old fool!" But God's grace speaks to his hurt and to his faith. God's challenge involves God's help.

The boy is the Son of the Most High and Joseph is adopted as his father. Into Joseph's bewilderment, pain and grief come peace, honour, joy and purpose as he receives the status of God-enabler.

Having seen, the shepherds return to their everyday world, of tending sheep but they have seen the fulfilment of God's promise, something they never imagined would include them, and their lives are changed forever. They remain poor, despised shepherds but, at the stable, they are given that special self-worth and dignity, which God gives to his children. Their work and social status are unchanged but caring for sheep will never be the same again, for they have met the Lamb of God. As they go, they share the story with everyone. The poor have good news for the poor. Those who receive the Evangelium (Gospel) are expected to be evangelists.

Lord, you must love ordinary people because you have made so many of them. May the Gospel be so lived and shared in humility and truth that they may come to see you present and at work in all our lives; that the earth may be filled with the glory of God as the waters cover the sea.

Questions for thought or discussion

1. The shepherds responded to the message of Good News by going to the stable? How do we respond?
2. The shepherds heard the great song declaring peace on earth? How is that song to be applied in today's world?
3. The shepherds represent the poor and socially rejected people of the land. How is the Good News to be shared with them?

Chapter Nine

Faithful Ones

O love the Lord, all you his saints! For the Lord preserves the faithful...
(Psalm 31.23)

At the end of eight days, the child is circumcised as one "under the law."[34] Then Joseph and Mary take their baby son to Jerusalem. Their visit is to fulfil two religious duties. The first is the purification of Mary after childbirth by the offering of an appropriate sacrifice, as laid down in Leviticus 12. Those who could afford it would bring a lamb, whilst the poor could offer two pigeons or doves. Mary and Joseph bring two of the birds! Secondly, they must go through the ceremony of the redemption of their first born [see Numbers 18.15-16: "the first born of human beings, you shall redeem. Their redemption price reckoned from one month of age, you shall fix at five shekels of silver, according to the shekel of the sanctuary..."] Even though this first born is uniquely special, he is taken through the due processes of the Law, just like any other first born "child of Abraham." In Jewish eyes there could be no better place for this obedience to the Law to be expressed and it is possible now only because they are in Bethlehem and not Nazareth. It is worth noting that Luke the Gentile, outside the Law and writing to Gentile readers, records the Law's requirements five times "according to the law" or similar phrases in this paragraph, thus underlining the strict devotion to the Law of Joseph and Mary. As they went through the ceremony, did they actually think that they could buy this child back from God?

This deep devotion by a young mother, if not by a young girl and her committed partner, is met by two aged people, who spend all their time in prayer at the Temple – Simeon and Anna, both of whom are filled with a sense of expectancy. Simeon is described as in the King James Bible as "just and devout"; 'just' is the same word as that used by Matthew in chapter one to describe Joseph. Interestingly, most modern translations retain the word 'devout', except for the *Good News Bible*, which says 'pious.' *The Interpreter's Dictionary of the Bible* states that in Isaiah 57.1, the word is a synonym for 'righteous.' In the New Testament, 2 Peter 2.9 uses the word to mean 'reverent, pious, devoted to the cult, whereas Luke limits its use in the *Acts of the Apostles* to worship offered by pagans, some of whom might have had some sort of link with the synagogue. Like Mary and Joseph, Simeon has been visited by God and given the promise that he will not die before he has seen the Christ of the Lord. Little wonder, then, that "he was waiting for the consolation of Israel." This phrase, in common use in rabbinic circles describes the fulfilment of Israel's hope for the coming of the Messiah. It was taken from the familiar words in Isaiah 40.1: "Comfort ye, comfort ye, my people, saith your God;" the opening fanfare of Second Isaiah (Chapters 40-55), on which Simeon draws extensively in his song.

Luke says that, "the Holy Spirit was upon him" and brought him at that moment to meet the Holy Family. Simeon is shown at once that the Messiah has come and that his long time of waiting is over, the promise is fulfilled: "Lord, now lettest thou thy servant depart in peace according to thy word." This is all Simeon says of himself – the work entrusted to him of waiting and praying is done; now he is released in peace. The Greek verb was generally used for the freeing of a slave by his master. The words are repeated all over the world each evening. He takes the baby in his arms and sings his praise to God. The fact that he held the child suggests that possibly he was a priest. In doing so, he draws extensively from the writings of Isaiah; Luke uses the Septuagint Greek translation. [35] At the same time, it is revealed to him that what God is doing is far greater than he or his people ever imagined. Until now, like Zechariah, he had awaited the Son of David, who would drive out the Romans and make Israel the supreme power. This child is the Saviour of all the nations, "a light to lighten the Gentiles, and the glory of thy people Israel." He echoes the words of Isaiah 52.10: The Lord has bared his holy arm before the eyes of all the nations; and all the ends of the earth shall see the salvation of our God."

According to the King James Version, "Joseph and his mother marvelled at those things which were said of him. Many Greek text speaks of "his father and mother," though some manuscripts name only Joseph. The old man turns to them and blesses them but then speaks only to Mary, for by the time the promises come to pass, Joseph will be dead. There is no reference to him in the main part of the Gospels of Matthew and Luke and he has no place in the family list in Mark 6. Simeon's message to her is far removed from the sweet and heart-warming words usually heard by a new mother. Her son will have no easy journey to his victory and throne. She will hear no tumultuous cries of acclamation. Her Jesus will be the Light by which the deeds, words, thoughts and feelings of the people of God will be revealed, especially to themselves. He will be a sign spoken against by the proud and the self-righteous and welcomed by the poor and lowly. There can be no sitting on a fence here. All must respond and all must be humbled before they can rise to new life in God's redeeming love. His words to her that "a sword shall pierce through thy own soul" would re-echo often through the years ahead as she followed the news of his journeys through the land and twist terribly during those terrible hours on Calvary.

Luke, with his respect for the place of women, gives Anna equal place. Her words are not recorded; nonetheless her message is powerful. Anna arrives just as Simeon speaks. In just three verses Luke paints her picture: Anna is the daughter of Phanuel, of the house of Asher. Her name means "grace" or "favour." She had been married for only seven years when her husband died and is now described as "a widow of 84 years." She spends all her time in the Temple, fasting and praying. Whereas Simeon is praised as "righteous and devout", Anna is given special status: she is described as "a prophetess," the only woman to be so described in the New Testament.

Simeon sings God's praise and speaks to Mary and Joseph. Anna tells other people what she has seen. Her words are not recorded; nonetheless her message is powerful but it is for a particular congregation, namely "those that looked for the redemption of Jerusalem." This phrase, like "the consolation of Israel," used of Simeon, refers to the coming of the Messiah.

The Eastern Orthodox Church regards Anna and Simeon "the God Receiver" as the last of the prophets and its icons of the Presentation of Christ often present Anna as standing behind Mary, when either her hands point to Christ to stress who he really is or show her handing a scroll, an image often used of prophets in such iconography.

These two are the last recorded people to see the child Jesus. This elderly pair, seemingly past their time of usefulness, represent the poor of the land. They join the shepherds, unclean social outcasts, and the Magi, unacceptable foreigners in welcoming him into the world.[36] "With the poor and mean and lowly lived on earth our Saviour holy."

God our Father, you kept faith with Simeon and Anna throughout their long lives and enabled them to live their lives faithful to you; help us in our turn, by your Holy Spirit, to know Jesus when he comes to us, that in all our living we may sing your praise.

Questions for thought or discussion

1. What does the example of Simeon and Anna say to us, especially the predominantly older generation in our

churches today?

2. Simeon and Anna represent constant faith. How constant is our faith?

3. What is the challenge or comfort of Simeon's song?

Chapter Ten

Four Songs

Not unto us, O Lord, not unto us, but to your name give glory, because of your mercy and because of your truth.
(Psalm 115.1)

Four songs appear in Luke's account of the Nativity: Mary's *Magnificat*, Zechariah's *Benedictus*, the angels' *Gloria* and Simeon's *Nunc Dimittiis*. Their titles came from the first word of each in the *Vulgate*. Saint Jerome (c.342-420), a Latin Christian is thought to have trained as a lawyer before his conversion and ordination to the priesthood. His great work was the translation of the Hebrew Old Testament and the Greek New Testament into the Latin of everyday life, the vulgar tongue; hence the title given to his translation. The Book of Common Prayer followed the practice of using the Latin opening word(s) for as titles for these songs (as it does also for the Psalms) and it is by these titles that they are now known.

Songs have an important role in most people's lives but familiarity leads to lack of hearing the message whilst prejudice can blind others to what is here. They can rouse devotion, love, hatred, patriotism and make people buy what they do not really want. All the great movements in Western history have their own anthems: the *Star Spangled Banner* of the War of American Independence, the *Marseillaise* of the French Revolution, and the *March of the Women* of the British Suffragette Movement. Later in the twentieth century came the clash of two ideologies: National Socialism with its *Horst Wessel Song* and Communism with its *Red Flag*. Then, no one can overstate the importance of *We shall overcome* in the struggle for Afro-American rights or that of *Nkosi Sikelel' iAfrika* in the long struggle against Apartheid.

Christians have used songs as war cries in their struggles against each other: in Protestantism, Luther's Ein Feste Burg, whilst Ulster Protestants sang *The Sash my father wore* to drown out the Catholics' *Faith of our fathers*. It seems worth noting that whereas all the other songs look forward, these two look back.

Among these forward-looking revolutionary anthems stands Mary's Magnificat, though so often it appears as though the whole Church seems to have forgotten the significance of her words, as indeed those of the other three also, turning it into a just another sweet song. Zechariah too looks forward to the coming great deeds of God, in which his son has a part to play. The angels' song fills the heavens with the praise of God for what he is doing now and what will come to pass because of that. Even the old man Simeon, in giving thanks for the fruition of his long-time of waiting and his release, actually looks forward to all peoples sharing the same privilege. These two represent all humble believers in every century whose prayers and faithful lives prepared the way for all the great movements of the Christian story.

So, all four songs celebrate the action of God in the birth of Jesus Christ, whose coming proclaims a revolution, whose lasting impact will be greater than all of the movements in history.

Praise be to God Almighty who, in his love, came to redeem humanity. Praise be to the Lord, who made himself as nothing to lift up the poor. Praise be to the holy Child born of Mary. Praise be to the eternal Word who became flesh for us. Praise be to Christ our Saviour, with the Father and the Spirit, now and for ever.

Questions for thought or discussion

1. What is the relevance of these songs to the Church and the world today?
2. Do songs have a place in our worship and our faith today?

3. How often do we offer pure praise to God, with no requests attached?

Chapter Eleven

Foreigners!

I will also give you as a light to the Gentiles, that you should
be my salvation to the ends of the earth.
(Isaiah 49.6)

The nativity stories of Matthew and Luke set the stage for the
major themes of the Gospel. The important folk of state and
church, such as Herod and the Chief Priest, are absent from the
scene. It seems as though they do not need good news. Perhaps
they believe that they are the good news. The shepherds are
followed by other visitors. After the poor of the land come
foreigners from the east. This is in keeping with the promise
made by God to Abraham in Genesis 12.3: "in you shall all the
families of the earth be blessed." The place of the nations in
God's purpose is repeated in the Old Testament and declared by
the prophets and especially Isaiah, who states that the Messiah's
mission is not limited to the Jews: 49.6: "I will give you as a
light to the nations, that my salvation may reach the end of the
earth." Whatever we make of this story, it has great symbolic
value as bringing east and west together, uniting the world in
God's covenant.

Shepherds are just shepherds but who are these? In the
English text they are described variously as wise men who
studied the stars, astrologers, magi. Matthew does not tell
us how many came but, as there were three gifts, it has been
assumed generally that there were three givers. Rich traditions
have grown up around them, which name them as Caspar, King
of India, Melchior, King of Persia and Balthazar, King of Arabia.
These men of different nations are said to be descendants of Noah
through his respective sons, Ham, Shem and Japheth. The idea

of kings is influenced by the words of Isaiah 60.3: "Nations shall come to your light and kings to the brightness of your dawn," and then in Isaiah 60.11: "Your gates shall always be open; day and night they shall not be shut, so that nations may bring you their wealth, with their kings led in procession."`

At the behest of this mother Helena, the emperor Constantine built five great basilicas in the Holy Land. All except one were destroyed by Persian invaders. The Church of the Nativity at Bethlehem remains. Why was it spared? If one enters the basilica and looks up to the right, there are the remains of a mosaic of men in Persian dress. It is said that the church was spared because the Persian soldiers who entered in the year 625 saw the mosaic and said that "those men up there look like us."

The Star

The Magi came, following a star. Stars were believed to have a great influence on human lives and events on earth. In ancient times astrological phenomena were linked with the births of great men, like Alexander and Augustus Caesar. According to the *Dead Sea Scrolls*. Bar Kochba, leader of the Jewish revolt of AD 132-135 was called "Son of the Star" and hailed as the nation's Messiah.

The ancient world around the birth of Jesus was in a state of expectancy, fuelled by what astrologers reported of activity in the heavens. There was a conjunction of Jupiter and Saturn three times in BC 7, whilst Halley's Comet appeared in AD 12. Something big was about to happen. Three men were led to travel a vast distance to the west, following their star.

In the Old Testament, the Oracle of Balaam (Numbers 24.17) declared that "I see him, but not now; I behold him, but not near – a star shall come out of Jacob, and a sceptre shall rise out of Israel..." Psalm 72.10-11 contains this hope and promise: "May the kings of Tarshish and all the isles render him tribute, may the kings of Sheba and Seba bring gifts, May all kings fall down

before him, all nations give him service. For he delivers the
needy when they call, the poor and those who have no helper..."

Eventually they reached Jerusalem and were given an
audience by Herod the King. After consulting his advisers he
directed them to Bethlehem and there they entered the cave-
stable of an inn.

The Stable

What must the three pilgrims have thought when their star
brought them to such a place? The lighting, if any, would be poor;
the furnishings fit only for animals and its odours far removed
from those of royal dwellings. In they went and found journey's
end at a manger in which lay a new born child. "So they went
into the house and saw the little child with his mother Mary.
And they fell on their knees and worshipped him." The order of
events is important. What is generally remembered is that they
brought gifts. What comes first for them and for everyone is the
worship, the offering of self. As the prophets keep repeating, this
is what God wants of us, most of all. Having paid homage, it is
then that they offer their gifts of gold, frankincense and myrrh.
As with all else in the accounts of the Nativity, these gifts have
great symbolic value.

First comes gold, always seen as fit for a king. 1 Kings 10.2
tells that when the Queen of Sheba visited Solomon, "having
heard of his fame," she brought camels loaded with precious
gifts, including "very much gold." Verse 25 of the same chapter
says that "kings of the earth" came bringing gifts with "objects
of silver and gold" in a prominent place.

Gold for a king is a symbol of wealth and the power it buys,
of livelihood, success, possessions and the desire for them. It
symbolises work, commerce, finance and politics. Kings brought
gold to Solomon, who already possessed it in great quantities,
together with political power and military might. Gold and all
it represents causes to much trouble unless those who use them

first offer themselves and what they have to God in self-giving worship.

These men freely offer gold to a poor baby, for whom there was "no room in the inn" at a time when the world's most powerful ruler was holding a census so as to force his subjects to give their gold to him.

Sweet-smelling Frankincense, which is second, is used in the manufacture of perfume or incense, a gift for a priest. I stood on a commuter train out of San Francisco once and the well-dressed sardines complained. A smart lady executive, squashed up against me, loudly sniffed the air once or twice, to my great discomfiture, before proclaiming loudly, "At least everyone smells alright!" What a relief! But what about our inner selves, our communities, our churches and our world? How do they smell?

Frankincense is the symbol of science, the arts and priesthood. Science without worship becomes chemical warfare and nuclear weapons, psychological and physical torture, technology with no concern for people or the environment. Among other things it leads to global warming. The arts without worship can become propaganda or pornography, expressions of decadence. Then there is the priestly gift. Even that can be used without worship, leading to ecclesiastical arrogance, denominational, theological or local church pride. The Church has priesthood in the world, worshipping God on behalf of all humanity, being pontifex (bridge-builder) between individuals, nations and races. It is Isaiah who has much to say of the promised Messiah - Isaiah 60.3 and 6: "Nations shall come to your light and kings to the brightness of your dawn... they shall bring gold and frankincense and proclaim the praise of the Lord." It seems clear that this prophet's words have a central place in the development of the tradition of the three kings.

Then there is Myrrh, costly and fit for a god. Exodus 31.22-32 speaks of the sacred anointing oil to be prepared by Moses to anoint the tent of meeting, the ark and all its other furnishings "so that they may be holy." "You shall anoint Aaron and his sons, and consecrate them, in order that they may serve me as priests... This shall be my holy anointing oil throughout your generations... it is holy and it shall be holy to you."

Myrrh was used as an embalming ointment and as penitential incense until the fifteenth century. It is used to give its scent to the holy oil traditionally used by the Eastern Orthodox Church at its sacraments of chrismation (anointing with oil at baptism) and unction and those who take these sacraments are described as "receiving the myrrh."

Myrrh in its bitterness is a suitable symbol of the birth of this child in a dirty stable in a dirty world, as well as of the way he must go in order to release God's redeeming love into this world. It symbolises a world in all its bitterness as well as the balm which heals it. Our wasteful generation is beginning to learn the art and science of recycling. The wise men with their myrrh, like the shepherds in their poverty, come to the manger where they too are re-cycled. The entrance to the Church of the Nativity is low; even short people must bend their necks to enter. The three kings, if that is what they were, freely bowed low before the manger because that is what they needed to do. Proud individuals, churches and nations need to do the same.

Origen in his *Contra Celsum* calls the gifts, "gold as to a king, myrrh as to one who was mortal, and incense as to a God." The carol, *We Three Kings of Orient*, takes up the theme:

Glorious now, we see him arise, King and God and Sacrifice.

Gold, frankincense and myrrh, valuable though they be, are worthless without worship. The wise men, symbols of a waiting, longing world, knew that Self had to be offered before their other priceless gifts.

Returning Home

Suddenly, it seems over for them and they must set out on their return journey. Their time at the stable must have seemed so brief, especially after the years of waiting and looking and the months of planning and travelling. There is a last minute change of plan "having been warned in a dream not to return to Herod, they returned to their country by another way."

Our Nativity scenes usually end with the Kings offering their gifts. But is that the end of their story or only its beginning? Does their behaviour match that of the shepherds? As they stop each evening on their long journey home, do they tell their story? Almost forty years pass before evangelists travel eastward with their good news of Jesus Christ. They found communities of people across the Middle East who welcomed them, because they had already been told. A thousand years later the Venetian Marco Polo (1254-1324), travelled three times overland to China, being away on his third journey for twenty four years. He claimed that he was shown the tombs of the Magi at Saba, south of Tehran in the 1270s. He stated that this city was both the starting place and end of their journeys and that they were buried in three large, beautiful tombs in a square and well-cared-for building, The bodies were intact, with full hair and beard. Communities treasured their oral traditions, keeping them safe by constant repetition.

Which route do they take? We are not told. Many of us like to return home on a different road, so as to have a change of scenery. Matthew tells us that they do so in order to avoid Jerusalem and Herod. But there is more to this story than that. Even if they had returned home on the same road it would have been by a new way. Their experience at the stable had made them different and they would see things differently. Matthew tells us nothing about them but, as we have seen, Luke describes the shepherds returning to 'every day', to their demanding work and inferior status, but they go "singing and praising God for all that they had seen and heard."

Lord God, the light of a star led the wise men to Jesus. We pray that by the Light of your Word and the faithful witness of your Church, the good news of your redeeming love may be made known to the ends of the earth, so that all people may come to you; through Jesus Christ our Lord.

Questions for thought or discussion

1. In the "Journey of the Magi" T. S. Eliot's wise men travel home wondering whether had seen a birth or a death. Comment.
2. The Magi brought gold, frankincense and myrrh. What are (1) we and (2) our generation doing with what these gifts represent?
3. The gospel story gives a place of honour to these foreigners. Where else do they honour foreigners?
4. How do we respond to people of Christians of a different background, to people of other religions or cultures and the sufferings of people far and wide in their poverty, injustice, pain and loneliness?

Chapter Twelve

Herod the King

Then you will say in your heart… I have lost my children and
am desolate… there I was alone… Thus says the Lord God,
They shall bring your sons in their arms, and your daughters
shall be carried on their shoulders.
(Isaiah 49.21)

"Christmas is the children's time," or so people say. There are,
of course, a Child and children in this story but the picture they
share is remarkably different from the Nativity plays so beloved
of parents, grandparents and adult congregations in general.

Herod the Great

Readers of Robert Graves' novel *I Claudius* and viewers of the
1976 television series of that name, repeated regularly since,
will have seen the young Herod as a popular figure at the court
of Caesar Augustus (Gaius Octavian). The Jewish historian
Josephus portrays him as strong, sensual and attractive and
an outstanding horseman, hunter and soldier. His noble wife
Mariamne the Hasmonean and her mother Alexandra were
fond of reminding him of his inferior birth and this probably
sharpened his great ambition and his vanity. One son, taller
than his father, said that he was expected to stoop in Herod's
presence and always missed his target when hunting with his
father, adding too that Herod dyed his hair black.

Herod's father Antipas the Idumean (Edomite) was a high
official in the court of Hyrcanus II, Ethnarch of Idumea (the
region between the Dead Sea and the Red Sea), whilst his mother
was an Egyptian from Alexandria. Though ethnically an Arab,
Herod, like his father, practised Judaism. Backed by Rome, he

became governor of Galilee at the age of 25, but his brutality was condemned by the Sanhedrin. He was hated by Sadducees for removing the High Priest and replacing him with his own nominees from Babylonia or Egypt. He appointed Aristobulus High Priest at the age of 17 but his appointee was a Hasmonean with a legitimate right to be High Priest - a genuine Jew, belonging to a priestly family. When Herod saw that his protégé was extremely popular with both the religious authorities and the people, he had him drowned. The Pharisees were angry because he ignored their advice when building the Temple. Defeated in a civil war, he fled to Rome, where he was an honoured guest at the court of Augustus. The Roman Senate elected him tetrarch of Judea in BC 37 and gave him an army with which to claim his kingdom. At the age of 36 he conquered Jerusalem and proclaimed himself king, becoming the unchallenged ruler of his territory for the next 32 years. In the conflict between Octavian and Mark Antony, he backed the latter, but Octavian after his victory, realising that he was the only man who could fit in with the Roman pattern. Herod received back Palestine as well as lands taken from him by Cleopatra of Egypt. Augustus (Octavian) later gave him parts of Jordan, Lebanon and Syria.

Herod was called 'the Great" because of his great building programme. He built two new cities, the port of Caesarea Maritima, named in honour of the Emperor Augustus, and Sebaste on the ruined site of ancient Samaria. He was responsible for the huge edifice at Hebron which covers the tombs of the Patriarchs, a place of pilgrimage today for Jews and Muslims alike. Herod engaged in vast building projects in the cities of Beirut, Damascus and Antioch. He constructed fortresses, aqueducts and amphitheatres. Herod's greatest achievement was the rebuilding of the Temple at Jerusalem. The 500 metre Western Wall of today is believed to be all that remains of the retaining walls around Temple Mount: these walls alone took 10,000 men ten years to construct. Herod's Temple, when completed, became the largest functioning religious site in the world and is still the world's largest man-made platform. The Jews were pleased to have the Temple but were not won over by its builder because his other works were largely foundations of which they could not approve.

For himself he constructed a series of palaces, each with a huge fortress nearby, in case he was attacked, his constant fear. These included Herodion (Har Herod) on its artificial mountain overlooking Bethlehem, where the palace at the bottom is matched by the great fortress at the top of the mountain. Most pilgrims who visit Jericho see only the Old Testament site but there is too a New Testament site in which are to be seen the ruins of Herod's winter palace with its fortress higher up the hill, whilst in Jerusalem he created the Antonia fortress. Masada, the last fortress to hold out against the Romans in the revolt of AD 70, was also his work.

Herod presided over a corrupt and decadent court. This roused the antagonism of pious Jews, who were appalled by what they saw. Particularly offensive to them were the spectacular Roman-style "heathen" games which he introduced, with their nudity and combats with wild animals. Some claimed that the spiritual and moral state of the priestly Sadducees was due to the pollution of the Temple during the rule of Herod I.

Herod's relationships with members of his family have fascinated historians alongside the fact that he was paranoid about those close to him plotting against him. To strengthen his legitimacy as King of Judea he married Mariamne. The fact that he was married already did not bother him and he banished his wife Doris and her son Antiper. In all he had ten wives, three of whom he had murdered, along with three of his sons and one father-in-law. His sixth wife was named Cleopatra of Jerusalem, so called, according to some historians, to differentiate her from Cleopatra of Egypt. Joseph suggests that the Egyptian queen "was overwhelmed with love for him," leading some to suggest that they had an affair but others claim that Herod's wife was the daughter of a Jerusalem nobleman, possibly of Jewish or Edomite-Phoenician extraction. She is said to have married Herod in 25 BC and borne him two sons - Herod, of whom little is known, and Herod Philip (later Tetrarch of Iturea and Trachonitis). This Cleopatra became the mother in law of Philip's wife and niece Salome. Philip and Salome had no children.

Experts have failed to agree on the nature of the dreadful illness which caused Herod's physical agonies and mental disturbance. According to Josephus, Herod was bathing at his palace at Jericho – when, in the heat and the steam he passed out. When his servants thought that he was dead, they went wild with excitement – and the noise revived him. He realised that no one would mourn his death. So he had the most popular men in his kingdom arrested and put in prison: he told the prison governor that when news came of Herod's death, he was to kill them, so that there would be mourning when the king died. His sister managed to get to the prison before that news and lied, saying that Herod had changed his mind and the men were to be released. So the Matthew story seems to be just another incident in the reign of this terrible man.

After the death of Herod, Caesar Augustus divided his lands between his three remaining sons. Herod Archelaus became ruler of Judea, Samaria and Idumea, but was removed because of incompetence two years later. The land became the Roman province of Judea with a Roman prefect or governor until AD 41; Herod Antipas (who killed John the Baptist) ruled Galilee and his brother Philip had the lands east of the Jordan.

The Wise Men at Jerusalem

This is the King who receives the visitors from the east. It is Herod who would speak first. He asks their business and they respond with a question, "Where is the baby born to be King of the Jews, for we have seen his star in the east and have come to worship him?" This is the gentiles' question. Later his Jewish opponents will call Jesus the Nazarene whilst gentiles write on his cross, "The King of the Jews."

Various translations tell us that Herod was "troubled, very upset, disturbed, greatly perturbed, frightened – and all Jerusalem with him." The Jewish historian Josephus records an interesting parallel in Egypt, when he describes how the Egyptians were filled with dread when told that a saviour of the Hebrews was to be born.

Herod's fear is quite understandable. It has been noted that he was always terrified of having his rule challenged, even by his own sons. This threat to the king appointed by the foreign power now comes from one "born to be King of the Jews." That is a major challenge.

Jerusalem too is scared. This is the home of the strong and powerful, the 'haves' in that society, not only in wealth and politics but in religion too. Any possibility of challenge is scary for them – and, of course, they have reason to be afraid even though they have not yet heard the radical message that this baby will bring, which "turns the world upside down!"

The king cannot answer their question so he calls in experts, the chief priests and doctors of the law. Why does he do this when, to say the least, he and the Sanhedrin are not on friendly terms? If nothing else, it can be a matter of "any port in a storm." As the Gospel account shows later, enemies do come together against a common foe.

It can be assumed that they consult their authorities and return with the word of the prophet Micah 5.2: "But you, O Bethlehem of Eprathah, who are one of the little clans of Judah, from you shall come forth from you one who is to rule in Israel, whose origin is from old, from ancient days."

Such confirmation of the visitors' words must have been devastating for all who heard it but Herod keeps his head. He turns to the visitors with a smile and sends them on their way with words of encouragement and a royal request, the kind that cannot be ignored: "Go and search diligently for the child; and when you have found him, bring me word that I may also go and pay him homage." Thus heartened, the men from the east set off, following the star on the last, short phase of their journey.

Herod waits for their return, ready to move at a moment's notice, to end this frightening challenge to his position. Days pass and the men do not return. The strength of Herod's fury cannot be imagined but he wastes no more time. He sends his soldiers to Bethlehem with orders to kill every male child under the age of two in the town and surrounding area, the sons of residents and visitors alike. Matthew quotes the words of Jeremiah 31.15: "A voice was heard in Ramah, wailing and loud lamentation, Rachel weeping for her children; she refused to be consoled, because they are no more." Rachel was a descendant of Benjamin and Ephraim. Her tomb stands at the road from Jerusalem on the edge of Bethlehem and was a place of pilgrimage for Jews, Christians and Muslims until recent times, especially for women who wanted children. Sadly access is now limited. Jeremiah's words are generally regarded as referring to the taking of the Ephraimites into exile in Babylon. Matthew omits the comfort offered in the words of the prophet (v.16), namely that the children will return home. The hope presented by the evangelist will be the major theme of his book. A terrible event! Little wonder that we generally ignore it at Christmas – it spoils our pleasure.

Why does Herod do this? The traditional and obvious explanation is that he is a tyrant, fearful of any challenge. Fearful of plots against him, he committed several political murders, including those of his wife and three of his sons. His subjects feared that there were secret police among them. Caesar Augustus said of him, "It is better to be Herod's pig than his son."

More needs to be said. The Nativity stories are full of

symbolism. Herod seems demonic – and symbolic. He is to be found in every generation in some part of our world, in the things tyrants, and sometimes others, may do in what they see as the defence of their countries or their own positions. He is to be met in our own fears of being swamped, overrun, manipulated, and threatened. We measure violence by who causes it and who suffers it, rather than the evil itself. Not long after the Iraq War I travelled on a magnificent highway from Aqaba to Damascus. It actually runs from Aqaba to Baghdad; it cost $68 million and was paid for by the American government to carry British and American arms to our ally Saddam Husain for his war against Iran. But whoever are friends or enemies at any one time, it is always the innocent poor who suffer. Why did Herod do it? Why do they do it? Why do we do it? Herod died eventually and he had solved nothing by his slaughter of the little boys at Bethlehem. He fails to destroy the Child. "The Light shines in the darkness and the darkness cannot extinguish it."

Loving Father, we cannot comprehend how innocent children could be made to suffer then – or now! We pray for children suffering in our own day, wherever they may be. Give comfort and peace to all who mourn the loss of their children. Give us the strength and vision to help all who are in need; for the sake of Jesus Christ our Saviour.

Questions for thought or discussion

1. People often say that "Christmas is the children's time." What do they mean by that? How does that fit in with the Gospel stories?
2. What does the Bethlehem story have to say to the world of today?
3. Does it give us hope? If so, how?

Chapter Thirteen

Refugees and Asylum Seekers

...the Lord of hosts shall bless, saying, Blessed is Egypt my
people, and Assyria the work of my hands, and Israel my
inheritance.
(Isaiah 19.25)

Though Isaiah's words belong to his prophecy concerning
redemption from Babylon they contain a general promise to
do with the redemption of Jew and Gentile - the whole world
including the nation which gave shelter and succour to the Holy
Family.

Egypt and journeys to and from that land have a prominent
place in the Bible story. It is a land of refuge, where first Abraham
and then Jacob and his sons are welcomed. There too Jeroboam
sought refuge from Solomon, returning to save Israel from the
yoke of Solomon's son, Rehoboam. It is also the land of bondage
and slavery from which the people are freed by Moses, who then
leads them through the wilderness, whilst Joshua leads them
into the Promised Land. All these stories have one theme, that of
God-given deliverance. This is the land to which Jesus is taken
for safety and from which he returns in due time. Twice Hosea
tells the people of the promise of deliverance - in chapter 2.14-15
he uses the picture of his fallen wife to present God's dealings
with the sinful nation: "I will allure her, and bring her into the
wilderness, and speak tenderly to her... There she shall respond
as in the days of her youth, at the time when she came out of the
land of Egypt" and in 11.1 where his picture is of a father and his
disobedient son: "When Israel was a child, I loved him, and out
of Egypt I called my son." Isaiah, in 40.3-5, cries out for a way

to be prepared in the desert for the one who is coming, when" the glory of the Lord shall be revealed, and all people shall see it together, for the mouth of the Lord has spoken."

In his second reported dream Joseph is told to "Get up, take the child and his mother, and flee to Egypt." Matthew here uses the Greek verb *pheuge* translated in verse 13 as "fled". It may be no coincidence that the same verb is used in the LXX Greek translation of Exodus 2.15: "But Moses fled from Pharaoh." However, in verse 14 the verb is *anechôresen*, meaning "departed," which Matthew uses on several occasions.[37]

One striking feature of Matthew's account is its similarity to the account of Israel's sojourn in Egypt recorded in the Book of Exodus.[38]

The Old Testament uses Egypt and Pharaoh to convey pictures of unbelief, hardness of heart and naked worldly power, a role taken up by Herod in Matthew. The killing of little boys by Herod is matched by Pharaoh's command to throw every Hebrew male baby into the Nile. Both kings die: Moses is told to return to Egypt with his family, whilst Joseph is commanded to return home.[39]

Some Jewish traditions declare that Moses' placement in the Nile was not only a demonstration of empathy with the plight of Israel: it was also the first stage of their salvation. Such traditions state that Pharaoh ordered all Hebrew male babies to be cast into the Nile because his astrologers told him that the saviour of Israel will meet his end by water. This prediction was fulfilled many years later when Moses was prevented from entering the Holy Land because of the "Waters of Strife." On the day that Moses was placed in the Nile, Pharaoh's astrologers informed him that the one destined to redeem the people of Israel has already been cast into the water, and the decree was revoked. As a three-month-old infant, seemingly a passive participant in the events surrounding him, Moses was already fulfilling his role as a saviour of his people.

So Moses is saved when other boys are killed by order of the king. Later, as a prince, Moses gives up all to save the people at God's command, just as later, a greater Prince gives up all to save all of God 's people at his command; at his birth the boys at Bethlehem die at a king's command. Moses is lifted from the Nile whilst Jesus rises out of the Jordan to begin his ministry.

Then Herod dies and Joseph prepares to take his young family home but another dream warns him not to return to Judaea for it is now ruled by one of Herod's sons, Archelaus. So in Exodus 4.19: 'The Lord said to Moses in Midian, "Go back to Egypt, for all those who were seeking your life are dead."' Moses tells the people (Deuteronomy 18.15), "The Lord will raise up for you a prophet like me from among your own people, you shall heed such a prophet."

Joseph takes mother and child back to Nazareth, where they are hidden away "in the back of beyond" for thirty years, just as Cousin John disappears among the Essenes for a similar period.

The nickname given here to Jesus has usually been written as "Nazarene, but "Nazorean" is closer to the Greek word used here. It is generally regarded as referring to the hilltop town in Galilee. However, Matthew seems to be following rabbinic practice in playing on words.

John Calvin, among others, claims that this word derives from a Hebrew word of similar sound meaning "to consecrate." Samson is to be "a Nazarite to God from birth,"[40] whilst Hannah dedicates her child to be born, Samuel, "as a Nazarite until the day of his death."[41] Other scholars believe it to come from a similar word, meaning "a shoot" and see it as referring to Isaiah 11.1: "A shoot shall come out from the stump of Jesse, and a branch shall grow out of his roots." Isaiah's Suffering Servant is described as "a young plant, and like a root out of dry ground."[42]

The words 'of Nazareth" are added to the name Jesus in the Gospels and later early followers of Jesus Christ are nicknamed Nazarenes by the Jews and are so known until the Gentiles of

Antioch coin a new nickname, "Christian", the name that stuck. Whether or not Matthew is deliberately comparing these three words (Nazarene, Nazorean and Nazarite), the similarities in his account of the coming of the Messiah would strike a chord in the minds and hearts of his Jewish Christian readers. Jesus too uses the story of Moses, as is seen in John 6.49-50: "Your ancestors ate the manna in the wilderness, and they died. This is the bread that comes down from heaven, so that one may eat of it and not die. I am the living bread that came down from heaven. Whoever eats this bread will live for ever; and the bread that I will give for the life of the world is my flesh." The same theme is followed in 1 Corinthians 10.1-5. Paul speaks of "our ancestors" in addressing a Gentile congregation to remind them that now they are part of the "Israel of God." The Corinthian Christians too must face a time of testing like that of their Israelite forefathers in the wilderness. The Hebrews were led each day by a pillar of cloud, symbolising the guidance of God (Exodus 13.21 and 14.19). They passed safely through the Red Sea, untouched by the water (Exodus 14.22). Their union with Moses was almost as though they had been baptised into him in the cloud and in the sea (1 Corinthians 10.2). In the same way the New Israel is baptised into Christ, who saves, guides and protects them. This is the grace of God, his love for those who have no claim on it. Paul maintains too that the manna, "the bread from heaven" (Exodus 16.4-35; Deuteronomy 8.3) is linked with the bread which Christ breaks in the Eucharist. Twice Moses struck a rock from which flowed water to quench the people's thirst – at Horeb (Exodus 17.6) and in the wilderness of Zin (Numbers 20.7-11). There developed a rabbinic tradition that this rock followed the Israelites thereafter, providing them with water. John takes up the theme of Christ satisfying thirst in chapters four and six; then in 7.37 Jesus cries, "If any are thirsty, let them come to me and drink." Later Paul states that the Lord Jesus "took the cup also, after supper, saying, 'This cup is the new covenant in my blood. Do this, as often as you drink it in remembrance of me." (1 Corinthians 10. 25). Throughout this section Paul's concern has been with the grace of God and the means of grace. He then proceeds to warn his readers that though the Israelites ate the manna and drank the water, they failed to respond to God's grace. So the Christians of Corinth should be ever vigilant against the temptations around them and their own inner weakness, for without faith, their sacraments would not save them.

Lord, as we remember the Holy Family finding asylum in Egypt, help us to remember too those who, in our day, are forced to flee from home, family and friends, to seek asylum amongst us; that we may show to them the same loving care as was given to the Christ Child in his need.

Questions for thought or discussion

1. The Holy Family found refuge in Egypt and the whole world has cause to be grateful. "Where is "Egypt" for today's generation of asylum seekers and refugees?

2. How does this apply to the situation of asylum seekers and refugees in our country and world, as well as the homeless among us?

3. Do you know what your country's procedures are for asylum seekers and refugees? Do you want to find out?

Chapter Fourteen

Growing Up

Train up a child in the way he [she] should go, and when he [she] is old, he [she] will not depart from it.
(Proverbs 22.6)

There is one story in Luke's gospel which seems, at first sight, to stand alone when, in fact, it links the birth and adult ministry of Jesus. It seems reasonable, therefore, to add it to the birth narratives. The only account of the first thirty years of the life of Jesus, after his birth, is that of his visit to Jerusalem when he was twelve. Jewish readers of the gospel would be thoroughly acquainted with what is being described. It has been rightly said, however, that Luke is not writing for a Jewish audience but for Gentile Christians, firstly in Asia Minor. They would be unfamiliar with Jewish practice, especially a generation after the events of which Luke is writing. This suggests that he is using the setting of imperial Rome, with its legacy of the cult of the Emperor, and also using the conventions of Graeco-Roman biographical writing to present One greater than Caesar. Whatever the case may be for that, Luke is presenting the story of a Jewish boy brought up in a pious Jewish family.

The Old Testament contained specific teachings on the nurture of children and it is obvious that Joseph and Mary followed them faithfully in the bringing up of Jesus.[43] Clearly, the Early Church showed little interest in his childhood, despite his teachings about children. When the disciples attempted to prevent people from bringing their children to him to be blessed, his response was firm: 'Let the little children come to me, and do not stop them; for it is to such as these that the kingdom belongs. Truly I tell you, "Whoever does not receive the kingdom of God as a child will never enter it."'[44] The gospels contain a number of stories of his own dealings with children.[45] These all point back to his own happy and fulfilling childhood at Nazareth in the care of Joseph and Mary. Luke's description of the boy Jesus is far removed from the pompous accounts of youthful precociousness found in ancient biography. Such writing was copied in Christian apocryphal writings as well as in art. An example of the latter is the painting by Holman Hunt, which depicts the boy Jesus on his feet, teaching the teachers in the Temple. The picture drawn by Luke is very different as he tells us that "they found him in the temple, sitting among the teachers, listening to them and asking them questions." This Jewish phrase was in common use to describe a student learning from his teacher.

The Law laid down that each Jew should visit Jerusalem on three occasions each year: the feasts of Passover, Pentecost and Tabernacles: "Three times a year all your males shall appear before the Lord your God at the place that he will choose: at the festival of unleavened bread, at the festival of weeks, and at the festival of booths."[46] By this period, the rule had been relaxed to ask for only one annual visit to the temple. Only men were commanded to attend but a tradition had developed which expected that boys should also be there.

Women often attended too as we see in the case of Hannah, mother of Samuel:" His mother used to make for him a little robe and take it to him each year, when she went up with her husband to offer the yearly sacrifice."[47] In the same way, the Nazareth family journeys to Jerusalem. They would walk with their neighbours, possibly a group from the local synagogue, just as churches go on coach outings today. The distance of eighty miles to Jerusalem would take three days. Their most likely route would be down the Jordan Valley to Jericho, from where they would climb up to Jerusalem. The coastal road built by the Romans and going through Graeco-Roman towns was unacceptable to pious Jews as was that through the hills of

Judaea because it involved crossing Samaritan land.

It seems that this was the occasion of his Bar Mitzva, his becoming a man according to Jewish Law. He would now be counted as one of the quorum of men needed to form a synagogue, taking on the responsibilities and obligations of an adult male Jew under the Law. To share in the Passover festival involved a stay of five days in the city before the party set off on its return journey of three days. It was common for them to walk in three groups: men, women and girls, and boys. The likelihood is that the new twelve-year-old 'men' would want to be together and so no one questioned where Jesus might be as he could be at any time either with one of his parents or with his peers.

The procession walked for a day before stopping for the night, when families came together once more. It is then that Joseph and Mary discover that their son is missing. Nothing can be done in the hours of darkness but, after a deeply troubled night, the couple sets out on the return walk to Jerusalem, with this walk too ending at nightfall. They spend the next day searching the city and eventually go to the temple where, to their great relief and amazement, they come across their boy.

The unanswered question is where had he been all the previous day and night and the suggestion is that he had been here, in the temple. At his age he would share the struggle with identity common to most children but this would be immeasurably more for Jesus. Something very great had led him to forget his filial duty to Mary and Joseph on this occasion. The comparisons between Hannah and Mary have been noted; there is a similar comparison between their sons, Samuel and Jesus, if one assumes that the latter had spent the previous day and night in the temple, spending the hours of darkness alone with his thoughts of God. During his years at Nazareth he has been growing into an awareness of the purposes of God and where he himself fits into them. He is in the process of realising that he is not just the son of Mary and Joseph, not only a son of Abraham.

He is just beginning the process of getting ready for his work of three years and his six hours on a cross.

He has been and will be under the influence of home, school and synagogue, learning from the teachings he received and the common life of ordinary people in his community. On the next day he approaches the teachers gathered in the temple to engage in a question and answer session. Their expertise is in the field of the Law, the prophets and the promise of the Messiah. They could explain their hope for the coming of the Son of David, the bringer of the New Covenant. Perhaps he or they referred to Isaiah's Suffering Servant but this seems less likely.[48]

Luke says that "all who heard him were amazed at his understanding and his answers." There must have been an audience or, perhaps, other people had been asking questions too but, by now, the boy was the centre of attention. The word *existanai*, translated here as "amazed" is one of Luke's favourites. It appears eleven times in his writings, whilst it is found elsewhere in the New Testament on less than half that number of occasions. Another word, *thaumazein*, used by the evangelist in drawing his picture of Jesus and in the response to him is "astonished," first used in the response of people to the shepherds' story. Yet another Greek word, *ekplessein*, is used to express the amazement of Mary and Joseph, and appears on four occasions in this gospel.

Mary is the first family member to speak, addressing her son with a mixed tone of relief and reproach. '"Child, why have you treated us like this?" She says what so many other mothers have said in similar situations: "Your father and I have hunted for your everywhere and we have been sick with worry." She addresses him as "Child" even though he was now a man, according to the Law, but mothers invariably forget such things, especially when worried. One may assume that he had never done such a thing before. He said to them, "Why were you searching for me? Did you not know that I must be in my Father's house?" Luke makes subtle play on Mary's "your father" and Jesus "my Father." His parents need to understand his words and his position. They struggle unsuccessfully to do so but, despite this, they accept and continue to shower parental love upon him. They are not the last to fail in this way. After speaking the parable of the Sower to the crowd, he tells his disciples; 'To you is given to know the secrets of the kingdom of God, but to others I speak in parables, so that "looking they do not perceive, and listening they may not understand."'[49] Soon afterwards, the disciples "understood nothing about these things."[50] The disciples understand only when he comes to them after his resurrection and just before his departure: "Then he opened their minds to understand the Scriptures."

Her son says to Mary that "I must be..." "Must" comes from his lips on a number of occasions linked with his life and death later on in Luke's account.[51] The Greek sentence used here for what he must be about has no noun and is literally translated as "the ... of my Father." This can mean either "in my Father's house or "about my Father's business." The King James Bible translation says, "Wist ye not that I must be about my Father's business?" while most modern translations are similar to that of the New American Revised Version's "Did you not know that I must be in my Father's house?

Jesus is speaking in the temple, so logic says that this is the more likely meaning. Where had they searched? Obviously they began among their fellow Nazareth pilgrims, seeking and asking members of each family and group, their own kith, kin and neighbours but they find the boy "in my Father's house." "Where else should he be?" is the implication. In his last week, he stands in the temple once more to declare of that place, in the words of the prophets, "My house shall be a house of prayer; but you have made it a den of thieves."[52]

The New Testament tells us of Jesus' attitude towards God, himself, people and the world around him, what he said and did and accepted. It tells us too how he was able to adopt such an attitude towards everyone and everything, how he was able to say and do and accept what came his way. It was by worship in synagogue, by personal Bible study and prayer, and by solitude and fellowship, all the things he learned in his childhood and youth. He was fed and led as a good Jew and human being and as the Son and Servant of God. The gospels use phrases like "driven by the Spirit" to say how he was fed and led. It was his special relationship with the Father, fostered and strengthened by all these means, which enable him to develop his special relationship with the Father's creation and the Father's children.

If it means business or work, he must first serve his apprenticeship and then work as a carpenter for some seventeen years altogether. Holman Hunt's painting, *The Shadow of the Cross* is to be seen in the City of Leeds Art Gallery. It depicts Jesus the young carpenter straightening up after hours of bending over his bench. As he stretches out his arms the sun shines on him, casting the shadow of a cross on the wall behind him. For this he was born – sent by God, to do the Father's will and to do the Father's work of forgiving, healing, redeeming, setting free, reconciling and loving. The coming years in Nazareth will be a sort of apprenticeship for that as he lives among people and gets to know them. He will work with his human father, "Joseph and Son, Carpenters," in preparation for fulfilling his calling as God's Son.

A boy had left Nazareth but he returns there as a man. Nonetheless, he continues to act as their son, obeying them. He practises obedience to his earthly parents; It is good training for the obedience he must show after he leaves home as he "fulfils the will of him who sent me."[53] Once more Luke tells us that "Mary treasured these things in her heart," just as others do about their growing children. This account ends, saying that "Jesus increased in wisdom and in years, and human favour." We have been led back to Hannah several times in Luke's birth narrative;

now the comparison is between the two sons, Samuel and Jesus. We read of the former, "Now the boy Samuel continued to grow both in stature and in favour with the Lord and the people."[54] This must be a deliberate action on Luke's part. Doubtless this described them well, as it does many other people who have later devoted themselves to the Lord's service. It must be said, however, that the boy in Luke's writing stands alone.

He disappears from view for some thirty years. When he reappears he goes to his cousin John at the Jordan, to receive his baptism of repentance on behalf of the people for whom he is to die and there 'a voice came from heaven, "You are my Son, the Beloved; with you I am well pleased."[55] Mark tells us that "the common people heard him gladly."[56] His hidden years of preparation served him well.

Heavenly Father, as we recall with thankfulness the parental care given to Jesus by Mary and Joseph, so now we pray for the families of this broken world, that they may be places of love and care; May his Church today truly be the family of Jesus, a community of reconciled and reconciling love, nurturing your little ones in faith, hope and love; to the glory of your name.

Questions for thought or discussion

1. Jesus is lost in Jerusalem, or so it seems. Have you felt ever that he has been lost to you? If so, how were you reunited?
2. What does coming of age mean for Jesus?
3. What is a mature Christian?

Chapter Fifteen

Fanfare

Praise ye the Lord... Praise God in his sanctuary: Praise him
in the firmament of his power... Praise him with the sound
of the trumpet... Let everything that hath breath praise the
Lord. Praise ye the Lord.
(Psalm 150)

The opening verses of the Fourth Gospel ring out like a fanfare or
overture, announcing the arrival of a great king. John's writing
is regarded by many as the high point of the New Testament as
it presents Jesus in the light of Christian experience. It succeeds
in bringing together the Jewish background of the story and the
religious language of the contemporary Greek-speaking world.
The author's purpose in writing is declared in John 20.31: "that
you may come to believe that Jesus is the Messiah, the Son of
God, and through believing you may have life in his name."
John is concerned to bear witness to the truth that in Jesus, "the
Word was made flesh and lived among us, and we have seen his
glory, the glory as of a father's only son, full of grace and truth."

Mark begins his gospel with the ministry of John the Baptist
and with Jesus coming to him to be baptised, the commencement
of the latter's ministry. The opening verses of Matthew's gospel
take the reader back to Abraham in order to introduce the reader
to "Jesus...who is called the Messiah." Luke opens with the
promise of this same John the Baptist but, later, in Chapter 3.23-
38, he takes us back to "Adam, Son of God." This is not enough
for John. He leads back to the creation and beyond it, to the
Creator. It is John who records the words of Jesus, "Very truly I
tell you, before Abraham was, I am."[57]

John does not write a biography and so is not concerned to

paint a picture of the birth and early life of Jesus. Nonetheless, it is John's Prologue which is seen as the pinnacle of the readings in the service of *Nine Lessons and Carols*, for which the congregation often stands. Instead, John provides repeated motifs, such as one finds in music. Both in the Prologue and the rest of the gospel, certain words and phrases are repeated over and over: "light and life, glory and truth." The theme of these opening verses is the Logos (the Word), who is pre-existent but becomes incarnate; though he suffers rejection by those who see themselves as the People of God, yet it is he who reveals God in his fullness and gives the status of sonship to all who believe in him. The evangelist's aim is made manifest in his opening words:

"In the beginning was the Word, and the Word was with God, and the Word was God. He was in the beginning with God. All things came into being through him, and without him, not one thing came into being. What has come into being with him was life, and the life was the light of all people." (NRSV)

It is surely no mere coincidence that John bases his words on those in the opening of the Book of Genesis. For him, the Christ (Messiah) is the Logos, the creative Word of God. His seven I AM phrases provide his pictures of Jesus: "I am the bread of life" (6.48); "I am the light of the world" (8:12); "I am the gate for the sheep" (John 10:9); "I am the good shepherd; the good shepherd lays down his life for the sheep" (John 10:11); "I am the resurrection, and the life" (John 11:25); I am the way, and the truth, and the life" (14:6); "I am the true vine, and my Father is the vinegrower" (John 15:1). In these phrases he spells out what he has introduced in his overture.

"The Word becomes flesh." He comes in the person of the man Jesus "to his own people" as their Christ and Saviour, but as the story progresses "his own people" choose hunger, darkness, lostness and death. That too is spelt out in the Prologue: "He came to what was his own, and his own people did not accept him. But to all who received him, who believed in his name, he gave the power to become children of God, who were born, not of blood, nor of the will of the flesh, nor of the will of man, but of God."[58]

In his story *The Country of the Blind,* H. G. Wells tells of a man who stumbles on a remote tribe of blind people. They only know blindness and get on with living in their darkness. The stranger tells them that he can see and describes the wonders all around them. Then he tells them of the greater wonder of the world beyond the mountains, where he belongs. His blind hearers cannot and will not believe him. They decide that the only hope for their sanity is to put out his eyes, so that he will become normal, like them. He escapes back to where he came from. But for the Christ, who comes from the Light as the Light of the world, there is no escape, for he seeks no escape. He goes the way ordained by divine Love. As he enters the darkness, so light is released into all the world. John's concern is to declare that the Light of the World has come. That "light shines in the darkness, and the darkness did not overcome it."

It is the First Letter of John which sums up the purpose of all four gospel writers in their own telling of the incarnation of Christ and what followed:

We declare to you what was from the beginning, what we have heard, what we have seen with our eyes, what we have looked at and touched with our hands concerning the word of life – this life was revealed, and we have seen it and testify to it, and declare to you the life that was with the Father and was revealed to us – we declare what we have seen and heard so that you also may have fellowship with us; and truly our fellowship is with the Father, and with his Son Jesus Christ... This is the message we have heard that God is light and in him there is no darkness at all... If we walk in the light as he himself is in the light, we have fellowship with one another, and the blood of Jesus cleanses us from all our sins.

What can we say in response to this – but to join in the angels' song?

Glory to God in the highest heaven, and on earth peace among those whom he favours.

God our Father: your Son Jesus Christ became a human being to claim us human beings as sisters and brothers in faith. Make us one with him, so that we may enjoy your love, and, as he lived, so may we live in joyful service as your children; for the sake of him who lives and reigns with you and the Holy Spirit, one God, now and forever.

Questions for thought or discussion

1. "Christians need to understand that the incarnation is not a matter of biology but of commitment, of deciding where they are going to stand." (Tom Arthur). Discuss.
2. What do adult Christians believe about Christmas? How does that fit in with what we have read in the gospels?
3. We hanker after strength of numbers and the power it brings – and we are brought to a baby in a manger, with no room in any human habitation. What does that say to us and the churches now?

Chapter Sixteen

Bugle Call

O Zion, that bringeth good tidings, get thee up into the high
mountain; O Jerusalem that bringeth good tidings, lift up thy
voice with strength; lift it up, be not afraid; say unto the cities
of Judah, Behold your God!
(Isaiah 40.9)

In my theological college in the 1950s we were taught that
whereas the Gospels according to Matthew and Luke contained
stories of the birth of Jesus and John had his great fanfare for
the Incarnation, Mark the first Gospel writer made no reference
to either but opened with John the Baptist and the beginnings
of the ministry of Jesus. *The Interpreter's Bible's* commentary on
Mark, first published in 1951, states categorically that "Unlike
the later Gospel of Luke, that of Mark has no preface setting
forth its author's purpose."[59]

Contemporary scholars have revised this view, stressing
that Mark too has a prologue, though there is some debate as
to whether it consists of the first eleven or first fifteen verses.
If John opens with a fanfare then Mark begins with a bugle call
demanding the attention of his readers to the proclamation which
follows: "the good news of Jesus Christ, the Son of God!" This is
Mark's theme. Though, at first glance, it might seem that his first
chapter centres on John the Baptist, this actor is merely the one
who is preparing the way, he and his ministry are subordinate
to the theme. The people must turn around to God and believe
the Good News.

It is generally believed that Mark wrote sometime between
A.D. 64 and A.D. 75. The world outlook was bleak. In A.D. 70
the Jewish 'underground' rose against their Roman rulers and

Jerusalem was under siege. Nero had died in the previous year and his death was followed by the assassination of four successors. Vespasian, commander of the forces attacking Jerusalem and then destroying it, had been crowned emperor. In Galilee there were tensions between Jews and Gentiles. Olive oil, a basic necessity, had rocketed in price. There was unemployment and social unrest. This evangelist writes for a post-Easter audience, whose readers could well have thought that this story ended with the death of Jesus. Many Roman coins bore a portrait of the emperor with the words, *Divi Filius* [Son of God]. Mark proclaims Jesus Christ, the Son of God." It is in him alone that the Hope of the World is to be found.

Mark's "beginning" refers not merely to his opening words or the baptism of Jesus by John but takes in the whole of the ministry of Jesus, his suffering, death and resurrection, calling his readers to share in the ministry, passion and resurrection of Jesus themselves. Matthew opens with the birth of Jesus; Luke begins with the birth of John the Baptist; Mark opens with the prophets proclaiming the coming of the Christ in the person of the man Jesus. He is concerned with the whole of the story of world redemption. John the Baptist is the promised Elijah, preparing the way of the Lord.

Nowhere in the first fourteen verses does Jesus utter a single word. First come the words which Mark attributes to Isaiah but which actually quote three Old Testament books. "The messenger" [Greek *angelos*] comes from Exodus 23.20, "Behold, I will send an angel [messenger] in front of you to guard you on the way and to bring you to the place that I have prepared. Be attentive to him and listen to his voice..." It is the prophet Malachi (3.1) and not Isaiah who takes up this promise in the first verse of chapter three: "See, I am sending my messenger to prepare the way before me..." Isaiah (40.3) is the prophet who describes the task of the messenger: "A voice cries out, 'in the wilderness prepare the way of the Lord...'" It is interesting to note that Mark felt free to move a significant comma and write, "the voice of one crying out in the wilderness, 'Prepare the way of the Lord...'" Both prophets are speaking to the Hebrews in Babylon of the end of their captivity. The people being told to prepare the way of the Lord would be familiar with the duty of Babylonian officials to ensure that every road in their care was ready for the king to travel on it. So God's people are called to the similar task of preparing his way for the Lord, who is at hand.

The use of a prologue was common in Greek drama and literature, enabling the audience to become aware of matters unknown to the actors on stage. Mark's Christ equals the Logos of John. His aim is to present a portrait of "Jesus Christ, the Son of God." The opening verse provides both a title for his book and the theme and purpose of his writing. As in classical prologues, the main actor is silent, so here Jesus says nothing: in the opening verses Exodus, Malachi and Isaiah speak of him; John the Baptist bears witness to him and God speaks and acts at the baptism. It is the Spirit which drives him into the wilderness where Satan tempts him and then angels minister to him. Only when all of this is at an end is it time for Jesus, the actor of our salvation to speak his opening lines: "The time is fulfilled, and the kingdom of God has come near; repent, and believe in the Good News." The drama of our redemption has begun.

If my memory is correct, it was Sir Malcolm Sargent who said something to the effect that anyone can sing the Hallelujah Chorus but it takes a great choir to sing the Amen. In speaking thus of music he made a theological statement of great importance. It can be easy for Christians to shout "Praise him!" when all goes well and especially on special church occasions – the Orthodox Liturgy of Saint John, Solemn High Mass, great preaching services, hymn singing festivals like those of Welsh-speaking Nonconformity, Pentecostal rallies, perhaps even in the deepest Quaker silence. It is surely another matter to whisper "So be it!

Here I am!" But it is then that the memory of the great occasions can give strength as we give ourselves to the Lord's will.

Mark's Prologue rings out like a bugle call to every Christian. It is time to wake up, fall in and move forward in the work of the Kingdom of God.

We praise you, Lord God, for the good news of Christmas. It sounds like a fanfare in our hearts. Let it ring out in our singing and our living as we respond to the bugle call of Jesus Christ our Lord.

Questions for thought or discussion

1. There are "great" occasions in church life which sound like fanfares. Have you experienced any? What have they done to you? What are they still doing for you?
2. "Amen is more difficult to sing than Alleluia." How does this apply to living out the Gospel message by us and our church?
3. Mark's Prologue rings out like a bugle call to the faithful. Do you think so? To what is it calling us?

Notes

1. Genesis 12.2-4
2. Exodus 2.24
3. Malachi 4.5
4. The King James Bible uses the English word covenant (including the phrase Ark of the Covenant) 24 times in Genesis, 11 in Exodus and 41 in Numbers, Leviticus and Deuteronomy; 17 times in Joshua and 3 in Judges.
5. Jeremiah 31.31; see also Isaiah 55.2 and Hosea 2.18
6. Genesis 6.18
7. Exodus 2.34
8. Exodus 34.10
9. Psalm 105.8-9: "He is mindful of his covenant for ever; of the word he commanded for a thousand generations, the covenant he made with Abraham, his sworn promise to Isaac, which he confirmed Israel as an everlasting covenant." See also 89. 3 and 111.5
10. Luke 19.41-44
11. Micah 5.2
12. Numbers 6.1-8
13. Acts 28.25-28
14. Luke 11. 29; 1 Corinthians 1.22
15. See Appendix
16. Verse 68 - Psalms 41. 13 & 111 9; v. 69 - 132. 17; v. 71 – Ps. 106.10; verses 72-73 quote Micah 7.20, Ps. 106.45 and Ps. 105.8-0.
17. A priestly dynasty founded by Zadok the priest during the reign of King David.
18. Matthew 11. 2-8; also Luke 7.18-23
19. Acts 1.8
20. John Buchan, *Augustus,* 1937.
21. K. C. Hanson, trans. *Census Edict for Roman Egypt*

22. Acts 5.37: *After him Judas the Galilean rose up at the time of the census and got people to follow him; he also perished; and those who followed him were scattered.*

23. William Barclay, *The Daily Study Bible: The Gospel of Luke, pp.* 22-23

24. Luke 2.26.

25. Isaiah 43.3 and 45.15

26. Acts 5.31 and 13.23

27. Isaiah 47.4; 51.15; Jeremiah 10.16; 31.35; Amos 5.27

28. 1 Samuel 12.9 etc.

29. Job 7.1 etc.

30. Numbers 4.3 etc.

31. I Kings 22.19 and 2 Chronicles 18.18.

32. Luke 19.38

33. Rev. Dr, James Moffatt (1870-1944). Minister in the United Free Church of Scotland. Professor of Greek and New Testament Exegesis, Mansfield College, Oxford, 1911-15; Professor of History, United Free Church College, 1915-27; Washburn Professor of Church History, Union Seminary, New York, 1927-39. His translation of the New Testament was published in 1913, followed by the Old Testament in two volumes 1924. The complete Bible appeared in 1926, with a revised and reset version in 1935.

34. Galatians 4.4 and Hebrews 2.17

35. Luke 40.5; 52.10; 42.6; 49.6; and 46.13.

36. The Latin 'Magi' comes from Old Persian. The word probably referred to a Zoroastrian priest.

37. Matthew 2.22, 4.12, 12.15, 14. 13, 15.21

38. Exodus 2, 15; 1.22; 2.23; 4.19; 4.30

39. Exodus 2.15; 1, 22; 2.23; 4.19; 4.30

40. Judges 5

41. 1 Samuel 1.11

42. Isaiah 53.2

43. Deuteronomy 4.10; 6.6-7; Psalm 22.

44. Luke 18.15-17; see also Matthew 18.3; Mark 9.34-37
45. Mark 3.12; 5.42-42; 10.14-16; Matthew 15.28; 17.18; 21.15; John 6.9-10
46. Deuteronomy 16.16; see also Exodus 23.14-27; 34.22-23
47. 1 Samuel 2.19 see also 1 Samuel 1.7
48. The late Professor Edgar Jones spoke of his invitation to speak to a Jewish group in a Yorkshire city. He chose to discuss the Suffering Servant and was surprised to discover that his audience had little interest in Isaiah's songs.
49. Luke 8. 10, quoting Isaiah 6.9-10
50. Luke 18.34. The other three gospels record a number of such instances.
51. I must proclaim (4. 43); The Son of Man must undergo great suffering (9.22); I must be on my way (13.33; first he must endure much suffering (17.25); I must stay at your house (19.5); these things must take place first (19.5); this scripture must be fulfilled in me (22.37); the Son of Man must be handed over (24.7); everything written about me in the law of Moses, the prophets and the psalms must be fulfilled (26.44).
52. Isaiah 56.7 & Jeremiah 7.11
53. John 4. 34. Such phrases appear many times in John's gospel.
54. 1 Samuel 2.26
55. Luke 3.22
56. Mark 12.37
57. 2. John 8.58
58. John 1.12-13
59. *The Interpreter's Bible,* Vol.7, page 633

Circle Books

CHRISTIAN FAITH

Circle Books explores a wide range of disciplines within the field of Christian faith and practice. It also draws on personal testimony and new ways of finding and expressing God's presence in the world today.

If you have enjoyed this book, why not tell other readers by posting a review on your preferred book site.

Recent bestsellers from Circle Books are:

I Am With You (Paperback)
John Woolley

These words of divine encouragement were given to John Woolley in his work as a hospital chaplain, and have since inspired and uplifted tens of thousands, even changed their lives.
Paperback: 978-1-90381-699-8 ebook: 978-1-78099-485-7

God Calling
A. J. Russell

365 messages of encouragement channelled from Christ to two anonymous "Listeners".
Hardcover: 978-1-905047-42-0 ebook: 978-1-78099-486-4

The Long Road to Heaven
A Lent Course Based on the Film
Tim Heaton

This second Lent resource from the author of *The Naturalist and the Christ* explores Christian understandings of "salvation" in a five-part study based on the film *The Way*.
Paperback: 978-1-78279-274-1 ebook: 978-1-78279-273-4

Abide In My Love
More Divine Help for Today's Needs
John Woolley

The companion to *I Am With You*, *Abide In My Love* offers words of divine encouragement.
Paperback: 978-1-84694-276-1

From the Bottom of the Pond
The Forgotten Art of Experiencing God in the Depths of the Present Moment
Simon Small
From the Bottom of the Pond takes us into the depths of the present moment, to the only place where God can be found.
Paperback: 978-1-84694-066-8 ebook: 978-1-78099-207-5

God Is A Symbol Of Something True
Why You Don't Have to Choose Either a Literal Creator God or a Blind, Indifferent Universe
Jack Call
In this examination of modern spiritual dilemmas, Call offers the explanation that some of the most important elements of life are beyond our control: everything is fundamentally alright.
Paperback: 978-1-84694-244-0

The Scarlet Cord
Conversations With God's Chosen Women
Lindsay Hardin Freeman, Karen N. Canton
Voiceless wax figures no longer, twelve biblical women, outspoken, independent, faithful, selfless risk-takers, come to life in *The Scarlet Cord*.
Paperback: 978-1-84694-375-1

Will You Join in Our Crusade?
The Invitation of the Gospels Unlocked by the Inspiration of Les Miserables
Steve Mann
Les Miserables' narrative is entwined with Bible study in this book of 42 daily readings from the Gospels, perfect for Lent or anytime.
Paperback: 978-1-78279-384-7 ebook: 978-1-78279-383-0

A Quiet Mind

Uniting Body, Mind and Emotions in Christian Spirituality

Eva McIntyre

A practical guide to finding peace in the present moment that will change your life, heal your wounds and bring you a quiet mind.

Paperback: 978-1-84694-507-6 ebook: 978-1-78099-005-7

Readers of ebooks can buy or view any of these bestsellers by clicking on the live link in the title. Most titles are published in paperback and as an ebook. Paperbacks are available in traditional bookshops. Both print and ebook formats are available online.

Find more titles and sign up to our readers' newsletter at http://www.johnhuntpublishing.com/christianity. Follow us on Facebook at https://www.facebook.com/ChristianAlternative.